# Predictability

Steve Bockman

**Predictability**
by Steve Bockman

**Printing History**

February 2013: version 1.1
February 2013: First Edition (version 1.0)

ISBN-10: 1482048582
ISBN-13: 978-1482048582

*To my mom and dad, whose steady encouragement
and support helped make this book possible*

# 1

"How long is it going to take?"

Bud Sanders had heard the question many times before, and hearing it now from his manager made him instantly uneasy.

"I really have no way of knowing, but if you'd like I can have a look at the specs in more detail, do some analysis, and get back to you as soon as I have an idea," Bud replied.

Bud and his manager, Bob Harvey, had been talking about a new feature for FiscalWare's flagship software product, MoneyMap. The folks over in marketing believed that the new FutureCash feature would drive the sale of many more copies of MoneyMap, a good thing by anyone's reckoning. But there was a market window inside which the most of those sales would be made, so Bob wanted to know if the new feature could be developed in time.

"I don't think that we need to do an in-depth analysis at this point," Bob said. "All I'm asking for right now is a ballpark estimate—your best guess as to how long it'll take."

Bud was still reluctant to offer an opinion, having been down this path several times before, both at FiscalWare and at other companies. "I'm not really comfortable with that, Bob," he replied. "There are so many things about FutureCash that I don't understand yet, I'd really rather talk to the whole development team and get their input before making any kind of commitment."

"Well, I think I can help you there," Bob said cheerfully. "Like I said, we're not looking for details. Just give me your gut feeling about this. We're not going to hold you to it."

Bud hesitated for a few moments while he considered his response. At last he answered, "Well, OK. Based on what I know so far, I'd say we're looking at somewhere around three months."

"Great!" Bob exclaimed. "That'll put us right in the middle of the market window."

"Remember," Bud reminded him, "this is just ballpark—my best guess off the top of my head."

Bob was already disappearing down the hallway, on his way to report back to the marketing group. Bud was anything but reassured.

*(one week later)*

"Hey, Bud!" a voice called out.

Bud spun around in his swivel chair to see the source of the outcry, Ted Russell, approaching at a rapid clip. Ted was the lead developer in the software department.

"Hey, Ted," Bud replied. "What's up?"

"I was just about to ask you the same thing, pal. What's this I hear about a firm delivery date for FutureCash?"

"First I heard of it," said Bud. "Who says there's a firm date?"

"Everyone, as far as I know," Ted answered. "The official schedule just got posted to the internal website."

Bud didn't want to believe what he was hearing, while at the same time he knew that what Ted was saying was possible, even probable. Just to confirm, he checked the company's website so that he could read the news for himself and, sure enough, there it was. His three month "ballpark" estimate that they "weren't going to hold him to" had become the official schedule.

Bud sat there in silence, shaking his head. It had happened again.

# 2

Jane Sanders listened without comment as Bud related the events of the past week. Seven years of marriage had taught her that Bud would need to tell it his own way before he was ready to hear any new thoughts or opinions.

"After I got over the initial shock," Bud continued, "I got up and hunted around for Bob Harvey. I wanted to talk with him about just *how* official the official schedule is, but his secretary told me he had already left for the day. After that I couldn't think of anything else to do, so I came home."

"I'm glad you did," Jane said. "After all, it's Friday anyway. I think it'll be good for you to get the weekend started a few hours early."

"The thing is," Bud remarked, "none of this by itself is really a big deal. Tight schedules are just part of business. I know that. There's always more to do than can be done in a given amount of time. This isn't the first time that I've been involved in a project with an ambitious schedule, and I'm certain it won't be the last. And now that I think about it, I'm not even sure what I was so upset about in the first place."

"You really don't know?" Jane probed.

"No. No, I guess I don't," Bud replied.

This was the cue Jane needed. "Well, I've got an opinion about that if you'd like to hear it," she said, "but I've got some questions I'd like to ask you first."

"Sure. I obviously need some help here," Bud agreed.

"First of all," Jane began, "does this situation, the business about your ballpark estimate turning into a commitment, seem familiar to you?"

"Well, yeah," Bud answered. "Like I said before, that happened all the time at my last job. In fact, that was the way most of the schedules there got created. Somebody would go around and poll everyone involved in a project, get their 'gut feel' about how long things would take, then somehow put together a schedule. It was pretty much standard operating procedure."

"And you're accustomed to doing things that way, " Jane stated.

"Yes, I suppose I am."

"I think so, too," Jane asserted, "so I doubt that this, by itself, is what you find upsetting."

"I tend to agree with you," Bud said. "Any other questions?"

Jane was just warming up. "Yes, one or two. If the situation that you describe is fairly normal, can you think of any problems that are likely to arise as a result of doing things this way?"

"Are you kidding?" Bud reacted. "It's going to be nothing but problems from now until the deadline!"

"Like what, for instance?" Jane inquired.

"Well, for starters, nobody actually knows if the deadline is realistic—not even me, and I provided the original estimate!" Bud said.

"So you're concerned about not being able to finish on time?"

"Yeah, that's part of it," Bud replied. "I guess I'm also a little worried about what's going to happen to me when we don't meet the deadline."

"I noticed that you said 'when,' not 'if.' Is that what you meant?"

"Yes, I believe so. In my experience, most projects don't finish on time, so I guess I have some natural pessimism built into my viewpoint. And this time I provided the estimate, so I expect there'll be consequences." Bud was growing more concerned as he thought about the implications.

Jane pushed on. "Do you foresee any other problems?"

Bud thought for a few moments. "Yes, I do. I haven't been at FiscalWare for very long, so I can't be certain about this, but if it's anything like my last job we can expect an increase in the amount of hours people are going to work. That probably means more than a few nights and weekends."

"Why is that?" Jane asked.

"Well, I'm basing my opinion on the idea that most of the people involved in the work don't believe the schedule any more than I do. If that's actually the case, people will start to put in more effort, just to have a chance at finishing the project somewhere near the deadline date."

"I can understand that," said Jane. "I assume you're including yourself in this night and weekend work?"

Bud thought for a while before he answered. "Yes, I am. And I'm not crazy about it, or about the underlying reason for doing it."

"What do you mean?"

"Well, it's like this," Bud went on. "I just now realized that part of the reason I'm likely to get on board and work overtime like everyone else is that I'm concerned about how it'll look, not only to the others, but to Bob Harvey, too, if I don't put in overtime while everyone else is sweating away. The last thing I need is to be held responsible for the project being late."

Jane noticed that Bud's concerned and thoughtful look was changing into the one she associated with resignation, as if he were about to make up his mind about something.

"What is it?" she asked.

"Oh, nothing I guess. I was just thinking about the software conference," Bud answered.

Jane knew what he meant. Bud had been looking forward to attending this year's National Software Development Conference in Las Vegas. He had begun attending that particular conference since sometime before they were married. It had become a tradition that he anticipated eagerly.

"Is that a problem?" Jane inquired. "You've made your plans already. Why not just go?"

"The conference is three weeks away," Bud replied. "We'll likely be in full development mode by then. Remember all that overtime we talked about?"

"Sure, but the people at work know you've been planning this, right?"

"Absolutely," Bud answered, "but I'm not sure that'll make much difference to them when they're working nights while I'm away on 'vacation.'"

"It seems to me," Jane ventured, "that a lot of what you're saying is based on supposition. How sure are you that all of this increased work activity is going to happen?"

"Oh, I'm not sure at all," Bud replied with a small amount of amusement. "It's just a guess—like my estimate was."

"Well, then, is there anything you can do to help lend a little more certainty to the picture before you make a decision about the conference?"

"Maybe," Bud mused. "The one thing that's missing in all of this is we don't yet have a real estimate of the work—just that silly guess I gave Bob."

"Can you make a real estimate at this point?" Jane urged.

"I don't see why not. The specifications were completed some time ago, and the work isn't scheduled to begin officially for another week. I should be able to knock out an estimate between now and then." Bud was starting to feel better about the whole situation.

"Good!" Jane declared. "In that case, how would you like to take me to see a movie?"

"Love to!" Bud responded, delighted at the sudden shift in direction the conversation had taken. It looked like it was shaping into a nice weekend after all.

# 3

Bud arrived at work earlier than usual on Monday morning, eager to get started on his detailed estimate. On his way back from the break room, coffee in hand, he spotted Ted Russell down the hallway.

"Good morning, Ted," Bud called out. "You're just the man I was looking for."

"Morning, Bud," Ted returned. "What's up?"

"I'm concerned over that goofy estimate I gave Bob last week, so I decided to do some deeper analysis and try to come up with a new estimate that has more thought behind it. I was hoping you'd have some time to help me with it, seeing as how you know more about FutureCash than I do. What do you say?"

"Well, I'm glad you mentioned it," Ted answered. "To tell the truth, I didn't much like the idea of being held to a schedule based on thirty seconds of discussion myself. Glad to help any way I can."

"I'm intending to start right away," said Bud. "Got any free time this morning?"

"Plenty," Ted replied. "The project is scheduled to start next week, and I'm expected to be getting ready for that anyway, so my time this week is pretty much my own. How about if I grab some coffee and settle in first? I can meet you in your office in fifteen or twenty minutes."

"That'd be perfect," Bud responded with some relief. "I'll go dig up the specs and start looking them over. See you when you get there."

Bud was even more energized than before. Ted had been involved in many more of the FutureCash design discussions than he had. Ted's participation would result in an even more realistic estimate, he felt certain.

Ted arrived in Bud's office seventeen minutes later. Bud noted to himself with some amusement that this was a positive sign of Ted's ability to estimate accurately.

"So how would you like to proceed?" Ted asked.

"I thought," replied Bud, "that we could start by reviewing the features and functions of FutureCash at a high level. You know—get the user's viewpoint so that we're both clear on all of the capabilities it is supposed to provide."

"Sounds good," Ted agreed. "Getting on the same page never hurts. Want me to start?"

"Yes, please do."

"Well, let's see," Ted began. "First of all we know that FutureCash will add functionality to the existing MoneyMap product. The new functionality is designed to allow users to see where their money is going in the future, and is intended to let them get answers to questions such as 'how much money will I have in the bank on a particular date?' or 'when will I be able to spend X amount of dollars and still keep a reasonable cash reserve around?'"

"And how will they be able to 'see' those things?" Bud asked. "Are we talking about rows and columns of figures, like in a spreadsheet, or are we thinking charts and graphs?"

"Both, really," Ted replied. "One of the views will look something like a check register, which shows all of the transactions that have been entered. Another view will be a line graph with dollars on the Y axis and calendar dates on the X axis. That'll be a way for the user to see, at a glance, what his or her money reserves will be over some period of time extending into the future."

"You mentioned entering transactions," Bud observed. "Is there some kind of form for the user to type in the transaction information?"

"Yes, there is," Ted replied. " The transaction entry form will have many of the same fields that a paper check has—date, dollar amount, payee, and even a memo field."

"And is that the only way for transactions to get into FutureCash—by manual entry?"

"Now that you mention it, no," Ted responded. "The spec also calls out an import capability so that users can transfer transactions from their online banking statements directly into the application, bypassing the manual entry step."

"Sounds handy," Bud said, jotting a note to dig into this a little more deeply later. He began to imagine a host of difficulties related to handling data files from a bunch of different banks, each with its own format, but contented himself for the moment with a written reminder.

Bud noticed another note he had written earlier. "I'd like to talk for a minute about transactions in general," he said.

"Sure," agreed Ted. "What about them?"

"Well, we already talked about manual entry of transactions, plus this automated import mechanism. Either of those methods should be fine for entering transactions that have already taken place, but that doesn't explain how we're able to see future transactions."

"You're right," Ted confirmed. "And that part of the application has already been specified—we just haven't talked about it yet."

"So how does it work?" Bud inquired.

"It's pretty straightforward, really. Remember that transaction form we talked about earlier? The user is able to indicate somewhere on that form that a transaction recurs on a periodic basis. I believe the spec calls for the user to be able to specify that a transaction recurs either weekly, monthly, quarterly or annually."

"Or not at all," Bud added.

"Right," Ted agreed. "Non-recurrence is one of the possible options—the default one, if I remember correctly."

Bud jotted another note, this time to remind himself to double-check the specs for information on recurring transactions.

"I've been wondering," Bud said, "what there was about FutureCash that made it sufficiently different from a standard spreadsheet program to warrant using it instead. Now I know. The ability to automatically generate these recurring transactions is enough to differentiate it." Privately he wondered if the marketing folks were intending to exploit this aspect of the application. He jotted another note.

"And that raises another question," Bud went on. "Is there something in the design that prevents an infinite number of recurring transactions from being displayed? For example, I pay rent every month, but I'm not likely to want to see that transaction listed over and over forever."

"Yeah," Ted answered, smiling. "That's an easy one. There are controls for setting both the beginning and end dates for the transactions in either the 'check register' view or the 'line graph' view. In other words, the user can elect to see only those transactions that occur within a range of dates."

"Yes, that would do it," Bud agreed. "Now, does that about sum up the capabilities we have to provide? Have we left out anything big?"

"Well we really haven't talked about some of the finer points of the user interface," Ted answered, "such as sorting the transactions by date or by payee name, for example. There may be a bunch of those small points that together add up to a substantial development effort."

"Agreed," said Bud. "We'll definitely want to account for that in our estimate."

The two men continued their discussion, going over feature after feature, with Ted providing the details as Bud took notes.

"I'd say we're about ready to start tackling the estimate," Bud suggested. "What do you think?"

"I think you're right. What do you say to picking up again after lunch?"

Ted was right—it was lunchtime. Bud wondered where the morning had gone.

# 4

Bud arrived back at the office in about an hour. Lunch had been pleasant enough. His usual practice for the midday break was to use it as an opportunity to get away from work entirely, both physically and mentally.

Today, however, was one of the exceptions. Bud had been mostly unaware of his lunch as he ate it, letting the part of his brain that governed such things run on autopilot while most of his attention was focused on the work that he and Ted had done in the morning, as well as the session yet to occur this afternoon.

Ted ambled in about fifteen minutes later, obviously relaxed.

"Nice lunch?" Bud asked perfunctorily.

"Fine, thanks," Ted answered. "You?"

"No complaints. Ready to get started again?" Bud hoped that Ted was as eager as he himself was to retain the traction they had developed together earlier in the day.

"Ready as I'll ever be," Ted replied. "Any ideas about how to proceed from here?"

"Yes, I think so," Bud began cautiously. "I was mulling this over at lunch and I think I've got a direction."

"I'm all ears. Go for it."

"Well," Bud began to sum up, "it seems to me that this morning we covered enough of the *capabilities* of FutureCash to paint a fairly complete picture, from the user's point of view. I'd say, then, that the next step is for us to figure out, based on that picture, what we actually have to *build* in order to deliver those capabilities to the user."

"That's sound enough, as far as it goes," Ted agreed. "Any idea how you'd like to go about it?" Ted knew that Bud already had an approach in mind, but was having fun playing the innocent in order to let Bud lay it out his own way.

"Yes, I think so," Bud went on, oblivious to Ted's amusement. "Nothing earth-shattering—just a fairly standard strategy of divide and conquer."

"Tell me more," Ted urged.

"It's basically this," Bud continued. "We start at a coarse level and identify the basic developmental areas. I'm thinking of things like user interface design, code development and testing."

"How about user documentation?" Ted offered.

"Yes," Bud agreed. "I seem to recall that the specs call for some kind of online user manual, so that definitely has to get done as well."

"And then we estimate how long each of those things will take?" Ted prompted.

"Well, we could do that, I suppose, but I imagine that will simply yield four goofy estimates in place of the one goofy estimate I gave last week. Not sure if that's helpful."

"You're probably right," Ted replied. "So we have to 'divide' some more before we can 'conquer.'"

"Exactly. We'll want to focus on each of those developmental areas and see how many tasks we can come up with inside each one. Once we have a reasonably complete set of tasks, we can estimate each one. Adding all the estimates together should give us our answer."

"Highly logical," Ted commended. "I do see a slight wrinkle, though."

"Only one?" Bud asked. "No problem. One wrinkle, I can deal with. What is it?"

"Just this," Ted responded. "I can see you and me doing the task breakdowns and estimates for the code development work—we're developers. But I don't think either of us knows enough about the user interface, testing or documentation work to figure out what those tasks are."

"Yeah, I see your point. You're right, of course, but you've also suggested the solution," Bud said.

"I'm nothing if not brilliant," Ted joked. "What solution did I suggest?"

"We just need to round up the specialists in each of those areas and have them do the tasking and estimating that we can't."

"I told you I was brilliant. Who did you have in mind?"

"Well, I'm thinking Marj for the user interface work, and George for the testing part," Bud answered.

"Sounds right," Ted concurred. "And may I suggest Carol for the user documentation?"

"Yes, you may, especially since Carol is the only doc person we have."

"No flaws in my logic, then," Ted wisecracked. "And I think we need one more."

"Who's that?"

"We haven't talked about this part yet, but there's another specialty area to be addressed."

"And what would that be?" Bud was genuinely curious.

"I'm guessing that a significant amount of the development work will involve accessing a database," Ted ventured. "After all, people will want the transactions they enter to be stored somewhere."

"No doubt," Bud agreed.

"So that's a specialty area we could use some help in, not only in the development of it, but also in tasking and estimating."

"When you're right, you're right. Got anyone in mind?"

"Yeah, I was thinking of Karl," said Ted. "I've worked with him on a couple of projects already. He knows what he's doing."

"Fair enough. Now we just need to muster the troops and let them know what we have in mind."

"Yup," said Ted, looking at his watch. "It may be a little late to get us all together today. Do you want to shoot for tomorrow morning?"

"Yes, I think that'll be our earliest opportunity," Bud answered. "I'll reserve a conference room for the morning and send out the invitations."

"Good, thanks," said Ted. "You know, I'm actually looking forward to this. Let me know if there's anything else I can do before then."

"I will. See you in the morning, then, if I can get everyone together."

As Ted sauntered off down the hall, Bud began booking a conference room. That was the easy part. Getting the necessary talent together all at the same time could often be somewhat like herding cats. He mentally crossed his fingers and started composing the invitation.

# 5

Bud arrived at the office on Tuesday morning to discover, much to his surprise, that everyone he had invited to the meeting had not only responded, but was also available to attend. He privately hoped that this lucky streak he seemed to be having would last until he was able to get in front of a slot machine or two on the upcoming Vegas trip.

When Bud got to the conference room, Ted was already there arranging chairs, erasing whiteboards, and generally prepping the room for use.

"Good morning, Ted," Bud offered.

"Right back at you, Bud." Ted smiled. He really *was* looking forward to this.

Bud wondered how a mundane task like providing an estimate could provoke such enthusiasm. Asking Ted about it would have to wait, however, as people were beginning to file in.

Karl was the next to arrive, coffee cup in hand. "Hey guys," he called out. Bud and Ted returned the greeting.

Marj and Carol came in together. Bud could overhear snippets of their conversation which had, as near as he could tell, something to do with shoes. Bud wasn't clear about whose shoes they were. The three men in the room simply smiled and nodded as the women found seats and continued chatting.

George was the last to arrive, drifting in a few minutes after the hour. "Sorry I'm late," he said to the room in general. "I was in another meeting that ran long."

That last was, in Bud's experience, so common an occurrence around FiscalWare that he had assumed it before George even mentioned it. Back-to-back meetings were common, and Bud wondered, not for the first time, what the overall effect would be if every company meeting always ran long.

"Howdy, George," Bud replied. "I'm glad you're here."

Bud was indeed glad, as George's arrival meant that all the invitees were present, and that they could begin.

"First," Bud began, raising his voice a little in order to get everyone's attention, "let me say thanks to everyone for making room in your schedules to attend this meeting. I realize that it was on short notice, and I really appreciate your taking the time to do this."

"Hey, if I wasn't here I'd have to be doing real work," Ted joked.

After the chuckles died down, Bud continued. "As you all know from the invitation I sent out yesterday, I gave Bob Harvey a ballpark estimate of three months for completing the FutureCash project."

Head nods indicated that everyone knew what Bud was talking about.

"The reason I called this meeting today," Bud went on, "is that I'm not comfortable with my off-the-cuff estimate becoming the official schedule. When Bob came to me he asked me for a 'ballpark' figure, which I ended up giving, but only with the understanding that I would not be held to it. Based on the information posted last week on the internal website, I'd say that we've drifted away from that understanding somewhat."

Carol raised her hand as she began to speak. "So are you hoping to gather some information in order to convince Bob to change the schedule?" she asked.

"No, not exactly." Bud replied. "At this point I think I'd be satisfied if I could simply provide Bob with a more detailed, and more realistic, estimate based on a deeper analysis of the project requirements. I don't know if a schedule change is possible at this point, but I'll sleep better knowing that I've at least attempted a realistic estimate."

"I'm curious about something, Bud," George piped up. "Have you spoken with Bob about your misgivings regarding the estimate you gave?"

Bud looked sheepish. "No, no I haven't. At least not yet," he admitted.

"Well, it's not my business really," George continued, "but do you think that might be a good idea?"

"Yes, I do," Bud answered, "and I will certainly have to speak with Bob about that eventually. To tell the truth, I've been puzzling over this very thing for a few days myself, and I think I know why I've been reluctant to bring it up with Bob. The thing is, I'm not actually certain at this point that my ballpark estimate is wrong!"

Bud took the ensuing silence as an invitation to proceed. "You see, it's like this—I've been imagining what it would be like if I made a big fuss to Bob over all of this, only to have it turn out that I'm an excellent guesser. It would be one thing if I wasn't sure I was *right* about the estimate. The problem is, I'm not sure I was *wrong*. I guess I'm saying that I'd prefer to have some facts in hand—one way or the other—before I make an issue about the estimate."

Nods all around let Bud know that the people in the room at least understood his position, even if they didn't necessarily agree with it. Things were going well.

Marj saw an opportunity to help move things along. "What did you have in mind, then, Bud? How can we help?"

"That I can answer," Bud responded. "Ted and I were talking about this yesterday and I think—we both think—that it would be helpful for each of you to do a couple of things. First, to break down the FutureCash project work that belongs to your areas of specialty into tasks to be done and, second, to assign a time estimate to each of those tasks."

"And then you'll total those to arrive at single, overall estimate?" Marj prompted.

"Yes, that's the general idea," Bud agreed.

"And how accurate—no, *precise* is what I actually mean—how precise would you like for each of these task estimates to be?" asked Marj.

"I'd say that estimating tasks in whole numbers of days will be precise enough," Ted jumped in. "Attempting anything finer than that at this point isn't likely to be that useful."

"Ted's right," Bud agreed. "And we probably don't have enough time for a finer breakdown at this point anyway."

Karl joined the conversation. "Speaking of 'enough time,'" he said, "how soon would you like to see these breakdowns and estimates from us?"

"Well, let's see," Bud mused. "The project is officially supposed to begin next Monday. I'd feel pretty good about this if I had a new estimate this Friday. That means I'd like to have breakdowns and estimates from each of you by close of business on Thursday."

"That's Thursday, two days from now?" Karl asked.

"Yes it is," Bud confirmed. "What do you think?"

A noticeable yet not uncomfortable silence filled the room for the next few moments as the various specialists considered Bud's question.

George was the first to interrupt the lull. "Yes, that's doable. I'm not involved in any testing at the moment, so I can get started on this right away."

"Thanks, George," Bud offered sincerely. "I really appreciate that."

"Count me in," echoed Marj. "I've got some other things on my plate, but I already know that most of the user interface stuff is spelled out in the specs, so I can get going on my tasking and estimates within a day."

"That'd be great," said Bud. He already knew that Ted was on board, so he cast an eye on Carol and Karl, who were both apparently still deliberating.

Carol was the first to respond. "I'm still finishing up some documentation for my current project," she explained. "I'd love to help out, but I'm not sure if I can have something ready for you by Thursday. Would Friday morning do?"

"Friday would be just fine, Carol," Bud replied. "Thanks! I know you'll probably be putting in some overtime to get this done."

Since everyone else had confirmed, all eyes now turned to Karl.

"Alright, I know when I'm outnumbered," Karl kidded. "Far be it from me to throw a monkey wrench into the works of this noble endeavor."

"I'll take that as a 'yes,'" Bud responded. "Really, folks, this is great news. I'm feeling much better about this already. So before we go, does anyone have any questions about what's needed?"

Marj volunteered to summarize. "What you're looking for are task estimates in each of our specialty areas. I'll work on user interface tasks, Carol will work on documentation tasks, George will concentrate on tasks related to testing and Karl will work on database-related tasks. I'm assuming that you and Ted will work on tasks related to code development. Is that about right?"

"So far, so good, "Ted answered for Bud and himself.

"Also," Carol added, "tasks are to be broken down so that each estimate is to the nearest whole number of days, meaning one day, two days, etc. In other words, no fractions."

"Exactly right," Bud agreed.

"And the estimates are to be ready by Friday, as early as possible," Carol tacked on.

"Right again," Bud confirmed. "Anything else?"

George glanced briefly at each of the other participants before proceeding. "Well, yeah, Bud. I've got something." He waited until it was clear that Bud expected him to continue. "I've been wondering about something ever since I received the invitation to this party."

"Go on, please."

"Well, it's just this...I got the distinct impression from your invitation that you felt personally responsible for the official schedule—the one that's now on the internal website."

"Yeah, I'd say that's an accurate statement," Bud admitted.

"It's just that I've been wondering why that is," George continued. "Bob Harvey came to me a couple of weeks ago and asked me how long I thought the work would take. I assumed that he was talking about *my* work, so I told him six weeks."

"I wasn't aware of that," Bud responded with surprise. "Did he ask you for a 'ballpark' estimate, or a detailed one?"

"Definitely 'ballpark.' I asked him for a day or two to work it out, but he insisted, so I 'guesstimated.'"

"I gave Bob a guesstimate, too," Marj chimed in. "Four weeks. And, like George, I also assumed Bob was asking me about my own work."

"I told him six weeks when he asked me about documentation," Carol volunteered.

"He didn't ask me," offered Karl. "But then, I wouldn't expect him to. How about you, Ted?"

"Nope, me neither," Ted responded, "but it would have surprised me had he asked."

A pattern was forming, giving Bud a clue as to what had taken place. "It looks like Bob went around to the department heads and asked each one to provide an estimate. That makes a lot of sense—I think I would do the same thing in his position. I just wasn't aware until now that he had done so."

"Well, Bud," Ted suggested, "it looks like you're not going to be able to take the blame for the official schedule after all."

"My thoughts exactly," George agreed. "I'd say that you, Marj, Carol and I each had a hand in this. It's the main reason I was so eager to attend this meeting—I'd really like the opportunity to back my estimate up with a few facts."

Smiles and nods by the other department heads let Bud know that they were in agreement. The feeling of relief that washed over him caused him to exhibit a sizeable grin of his own.

# 6

Bud and Ted spotted each other in the FiscalWare parking lot on Wednesday morning, both having arrived a little earlier than was customary.

Smiling and waving, Ted offered, "Well, aren't we a couple of eager beavers?"

It wasn't the first time that Bud wondered where Ted dug up these expressions.

"Howdy, Ted," Bud replied as they entered the lobby. "Yes, I guess we are. Ready to start right in?"

"You bet. How about your office in fifteen minutes?"

"I was thinking we'd grab a conference room again if one is available," Bud responded. "I have a feeling we'll need a whiteboard."

"Good idea. OK, want to text me when you've got one lined up?" Ted asked.

"Yup. Let me see what I can find." With that, the two men parted ways, Bud heading for his office and Ted for his cubicle by way of the break room to pick up a cup of coffee.

Twenty minutes later, the two converged on the one conference room that was still available that morning. Each had brought his own laptop, and Ted was also carrying a printed copy of the FutureCash requirements document.

"Thought this might be handy for scribbling some notes," Ted explained.

Bud smiled and nodded without comment as he set up a place to work. Ted busied himself with erasing whiteboards. A few minutes later, both were ready to begin.

"How would you like to start?" Ted asked, letting Bud take the lead on the meeting's structure.

Bud grinned. "Glad you asked. I've been thinking about this, and it seems to me that we have two main things to accomplish before Friday. First, there's the task breakdown or, in other words, finding out in sufficient detail what it is we have to *do*. Second, there's assigning a number of days to each task."

"Yeah, that's what we talked about before," Ted agreed. "So are you thinking about breaking out each task and assigning an estimate to it, or do you want to do all of the task breakdown first, and then do all of the estimates in a second pass?"

"I'm not one hundred percent certain," Bud replied cautiously. "I can see doing it either way, but the second approach you mentioned feels better to me somehow. I'm thinking that the task breakdown itself may require multiple passes, so there's a potential for doing a lot of unnecessary re-estimation before we get the task breakdown where we like it. I guess I'd like to just concentrate on the breakdown to start."

"Suits me," said Ted. "That seems the simpler of the two approaches."

"Good, then let's get started. Feel like tackling 'transactions' first?"

"That's as good a place to start as any," Ted answered. "Everything in FutureCash seems to be centered around the concept of a *transaction*. Users will enter them, view them update them, delete them and sort them."

"That's how I see it," Bud concurred. "How about starting with the work related to entering transactions?"

"Sure, just let me look at the specs for a minute," Ted answered. After a few brief moments he continued, "Oh, yeah, we talked about this just the other day. The specs call for a data-entry form that lets the user enter all of the parts of a transaction—date, amount, payee, a memo—stuff like that."

"So I'd say that 'create transaction entry form' sounds like one of our tasks," Bud offered, jotting on the whiteboard as he spoke.

"Me too," Ted agreed. "And assuming that means a *functioning* entry form, rather than something that just looks like a form, we'll have to write code to process whatever the user enters in each of the fields."

Bud liked the momentum they seemed to be gaining. "Well, let's just take them one at a time, then," he suggested. "What do we have to do to implement a functioning *date* field?"

"Hang on a second." Ted scanned the requirements document until he found the appropriate specification. "Says here that there's some special behavior associated with that field. First, there's the standard kind of validation you would expect—in other words, the field must contain a valid date. The system squawks if the date isn't valid."

"So we could make 'validate date field' one of our tasks."

"Sounds right," Ted agreed. "Also, the spec says that the user should be able to enter 'shorthand' date values—for example, '6/1' instead of the longer '06/01/2013'—and the software should convert what the user entered to a standard format."

"Makes sense," Bud commented. "Let's make another task— 'convert date field contents to standard format.' Anything else we need to do with the date field?"

"No, I think that covers it," Ted answered. "Let's move on to the *amount* field."

"This is just a straightforward dollar amount, right?" Bud inquired.

"Yep. Two decimal places. No dollar sign necessary. There's the standard validation, of course."

"Right," Bud said. "I'll capture that as 'validate amount field.'"

"There's more to it," Ted continued. "The spec says that, like with the date field, the user can enter a 'shorthand' value. The example given is that the user enters '12.3', which the software interprets and converts to '12.30'."

"Sounds like spreadsheet behavior," Bud commented. "I like that. I'll record that as 'convert amount field contents to standard format.' Anything else?"

"Yeah, here's something interesting," Ted replied, his nose still in the requirements document. "To understand this, it's important to remember that a *transaction* can represent either a debit or credit to the user's supply of cash. The same *amount* field is used for both purposes. That means a positive value indicates a credit, while a negative value indicates a debit."

"That makes sense," Bud responded. "Where's the 'interesting' part?"

"'Patience, Grasshopper,'" Ted counseled. "The interesting part is that the spec calls for alternate ways for the user to specify whether a transaction is a debit or credit. The most direct is for the user to simply enter the minus sign to signify a debit."

"OK. What's the alternative?" Bud was enjoying learning about the software in this fashion.

"The user can indicate a debit by clicking a 'debit' button, and a credit by clicking a 'credit' button. They're mutually exclusive of course—like radio buttons. Clicking one turns off the other."

"I can see that," Bud said. "I can also envision some interaction between the pair of buttons and the *amount* field itself."

"Yes, that's right," Ted went on. "For instance, if the user enters a negative value into the *amount* field, the software should automatically select the 'debit' button—that's in the spec."

"Likewise," Bud conjectured, "if the user enters a positive value in the *amount* field and then clicks the 'debit' button, the software automatically inserts a minus sign in the *amount* field."

"Yep, that's in there, too." Ted confirmed.

"I think we understand this," Bud declared. "I'm capturing this as 'implement amount field/button interaction.' Okay with you?"

"Yeah, that's fine. I think that's enough of a reminder that we'll understand it when we get around to estimating it."

"Let's have a look at the next field, then," Bud suggested. "Which one would that be?"

"The next field in the spec is called *payer/payee*," Ted answered.

"That's one field?" Bud seemed a little surprised.

"Yes, the spec indicates that the user can enter either the payer name or the payee name in that field. The distinction depends on whether the transaction is a debit or a credit," Ted replied.

"Oh, of course, that makes perfect sense. Sorry—I'm a little slow sometimes. Anything special about the field?"

"Yeah, this is a fun one. Based on the assumption that the user will eventually enter many transactions with the same payer or payee name, the spec calls for 'incremental search' behavior on the field."

"'Incremental search?'"

"Yeah, that's what they call it." Ted smiled, remembering his own puzzlement when he first heard the term. "You've seen this before—you're typing text into a box, and a list pops up containing suggestions that you can select from. It's intended to make it so the user doesn't have to type in the whole payer or payee every time."

"Oh, that!" Bud exclaimed. "I see those everywhere—just didn't know what the were called. I'll capture that as 'implement incremental search on payer/payee field.' Any special validation required for this one?"

"Let's see," replied Ted, eyeing the spec. "No, it looks like any text is valid there."

"Good," Bud replied. "Let's keep going."

Ted was slightly ahead of him. "Next there's a *memo* field. It's pure text, like *payer/payee*, and is intended to let the user enter a note about the transaction."

"Seems straightforward enough," Bud said. "Any 'incremental search' on this one?"

Ted consulted the requirements document. "Well, I didn't think so, but the spec says yes. Ah, here it is—the assumption is that there may be a lot of reuse. For example, the user might type 'groceries' into this field, and it would be handy to have that selectable from the list when the next 'groceries' transaction gets entered."

"Yeah, that makes sense," Bud agreed. "Let me record that as 'implement incremental search on memo field.' Is that it?"

"No, not quite," Ted replied. "There's another one—the *recurrence* selector.

"Not a data-entry field, then," Bud clarified.

"No, that's right. This is a collection of radio buttons that allows the user to specify how often a transaction recurs. The spec says the choices should be *never, weekly, semi-monthly, monthly, quarterly* and *yearly*. The default selection is *never*, which is another way of saying it's a one-time transaction."

"I follow that," said Bud. "I'm going to capture that as 'implement recurrence selector.' So are we done with the transaction form?"

"Well," Ted replied, "there is supposed to be a button on the form that allows the user to add the transaction to the collection of transactions once all the fields are filled in."

"Better grab that, too," Bud said while jotting it on the whiteboard. "'Implement add button.'"

"And I think that's it," Ted offered.

"Very nice." Bud grinned. This was going well. "Want to keep going?"

"That's what I'm here for, chief," Ted replied cheerfully. "How about if we tackle the 'check register' view next? That's the gadget that displays a bunch of transactions, spreadsheet style."

"Yeah, that makes sense. We've given the user the ability to record transactions—it's safe to assume that he or she would like to see them."

"My thoughts exactly," Ted agreed. "First we'll need the ability to display all of the fields of a transaction in a single row. The column headings can hold the names of the fields."

Bud was already busy writing. "I'm recording that as 'implement display of single transaction.'"

"Right," Ted agreed. "Next we'll want to..."

The two had found their rhythm. For the next several hours, anyone who happened to look into the conference room would have seen the pair happily at work, engaging in animated discussions and jotting notes on the whiteboard as they went about the business of turning the FutureCash requirements into code development tasks.

# 7

When Bud checked his e-mail Friday morning, he was pleased to discover that everyone was ready with an estimate. Even Carol, who had thought she would need a little extra time to complete the task, had finished ahead of her own schedule. Bud reflected, and not for the first time, that if everyone could estimate *work* as accurately as they estimated *estimates*, there would be little trouble in predicting the project completion date.

"Time to round up the troops," Bud thought as he began composing the invitation. He was eager, even a little nervous, to see what the final tally would be.

This time it was Karl's turn to be late to the meeting. Karl didn't verbalize any excuse, but offered a smile and a shrug to acknowledge his tardiness.

"Thanks for coming, everyone," Bud began. "We all know why we're here—it's time to share our estimates for the various kinds of work to be done on the FutureCash project. Everyone here has already indicated that their estimates are ready, so let's begin. How about if we start with user experience? Marj, would you like to go first?"

"Sure, Bud," Marj responded. "How would you like the information?"

Bud pondered the question for a brief moment. "Well, why don't you share with us the total number of tasks you came up with, as well as the total estimate. We can go into details later if we need to."

"No problem," Marj replied. "I broke the user experience work into 5 tasks, and I estimated they would take a total of 25 days."

"So your average task is about 5 days in length," Bud clarified.

"Yes, that's right," Marj confirmed. "It turned out that there are 5 major areas of user interface to design, and I estimated each one of those as a week's work. Therefore 25 days."

"OK, thanks, Marj. Ted, would you like to report on the work that you and I did?"

"Glad to," Ted replied, referring to some notes he'd brought with him. "For the code development work, Bud and I were able to come up with 55 major tasks, for a total estimate of 71 days."

"Thanks, Ted," Bud said as he added Ted's figures to the whiteboard. "Karl, I think you're next. I know that Bob didn't ask you for an estimate originally. What did you come up with?"

"Glad someone *did* ask," Karl acknowledged. "I came up with what seems like a fairly significant estimate—6 database design tasks, for a total of 15 days."

"Alright, thanks," Bud replied as he jotted down the new figures. "George? Let's hear about estimates for testing."

"I've got 35 tasks and 35 days," George offered.

"Hey, that's intriguing," Ted interjected. "How did that happen?"

"It's not the coincidence it appears to be," George responded. "When I did my first round of breakdowns and estimates, I had a whole bunch of tasks that were each less than a day—some only an hour or two each. It was a fairly simple matter to combine those into 1-day chunks, so that's what I did. And that's why I got 35 for both."

"I follow you," replied Ted. "Thanks for clearing that up."

"Carol, I think that leaves just you," Bud said. "What have you got for us?"

"I came up with 18 distinct documentation tasks of a day or two each, for a total of 24 days," Carol offered.

"Very good. Thanks, Carol," Bud replied as he began to total the figures on the board. "Someone check me on this—if my addition is correct, that gives us 119 total tasks, with a total estimate of 170 days. Is that right?"

A small flurry of activity ensued as half of the people in the room double-checked Bud's figures using paper and pencil, while the other half punched numbers into smartphone calculators.

"Yep, that's right!"

"I agree!"

"That's what I got!"

Eyeing the whiteboard, the group pondered the figures for several moments, attempting to take in the new information.

Ted was the first to break the silence. "Are we saying that the project is going to take six months?" he asked.

"No, it's worse than that," Karl sighed. "The 170 figure represents *workdays*, not calendar days. How many workdays are there in a month?"

"On average, 21.7," George responded. "I happened to make that calculation when I was doing my estimating."

"So how many months are we really talking about?" asked Ted.

Some more quick calculating yielded an answer. "If there are 21.7 workdays in a month, then we're talking about 7.8 months," George declared.

After a brief but rather uncomfortable silence, Carol asked, "Are we really saying that our three-month project is going to take almost eight months?"

Bud waited just a bit before jumping in. He had thought about this quite a lot over the past few days. Smiling, he said, "No, I don't think that's what we're saying. It *would* be if we worked in a completely linear way—first do all the user experience work, then all the code development, then all the testing, etc.—but we don't. In fact, for the most part, we'll all be working on our own portions of the project at the same time."

"Well, assuming that kind of parallelism," Karl asked, "what kind of calendar time do you think we're actually looking at?"

Bud turned to the whiteboard and studied the figures there. "I'd say," he suggested at last, "that we're largely interested in the work that takes the most time. That's code development, estimated at 71 days. What's that in months?"

George was the first to respond. "That's 3.3 months, Bud. We're supposed to be done in 3."

"I'm completely happy with that," Bud said with obvious relief. "My main concern coming into this meeting was that one of your estimates would be larger than the one that Ted and I came up with. This information shows that we think we're within about ten percent of hitting our deadline. That's good news—and, who knows, we might even be able to trim some of the fat after the project is underway."

Bud's optimism was infectious, as evidenced by the round of cheers and high-fives offered by the other members of the group.

As the congratulations subsided and people began to file out, Bud realized that he was going to be able to attend that conference after all.

"Cool," he thought. "Las Vegas, here I come!"

# 8

"Do you need for me to drive you to the airporter in the morning?" Jane Sanders asked as she watched Bud pack.

"No, thanks," Bud answered. "I'm planning to call a cab. No sense in both of us having to get up early."

Bud and Jane lived about ninety minutes away from San Francisco International airport. It was Bud's practice to take the airporter rather than drive in and park his car, especially for longer trips.

"Did you pack a jacket?"

"Uh, no. I'm guessing it'll be pretty hot in Vegas," Bud replied.

"Well, a really smart person once told me 'better to have it and not need it than to need it and not have it.'"

Bud smiled at the familiar quote, having uttered it himself countless times in the past. Heeding his own advice, he went to find his jacket and added it to the suitcase.

"I'm glad you decided to take this trip after all," Jane said. "The break will do you good, and I know how much you enjoy this conference."

"I'm glad, too," Bud agreed. "And you're right—it'll be nice to get away from work for a bit and clear my head. There will certainly be plenty to do when I get back, and I like the idea of coming back refreshed."

"Ready to turn in? Got your alarm set?"

"Yes to both," Bud answered.

Jane turned on the TV and switched off the bedroom light as Bud got ready for bed. They made it about halfway through an old, familiar science fiction film before drifting off.

• • • • •

The flight from SFO to McCarran International was just the way Bud liked it—uneventful. With the exception of the standard turbulence that seemed, more often than not, to coincide with the beverage service, the flight was a smooth one.

Although he had managed to get a little work done on the airporter that morning, Bud didn't even open his laptop on the plane, preferring instead to gaze out the window and generally enjoy the experience of flight. He preferred flying during the day so that he could watch the terrain and spot interesting cloud formations while 'helping the pilot keep the wings level.' Bud found night flying mildly disorienting, and was glad he had been able to find a daytime flight.

After just a little over an hour in the air, a flight attendant announced that the descent into Las Vegas was about to begin. Obediently placing his seat-back and tray table in the upright and locked position, Bud began to speculate warmly about the next three days. This conference had long been his favorite annual event, and he was happy to be able to attend again this year.

Shortly after touchdown, Bud texted Jane that he had arrived safely in Las Vegas. Disembarking the aircraft was the usual slow procedure, but Bud was in no hurry. Registration didn't begin until the next day, so he didn't feel rushed.

Bud ambled through the concourse, following signs that directed travelers to the baggage claim area. He had been in this terminal more than once in the past few years, but still he occasionally stopped to marvel at the vast array of slot machines that seemed to occupy every cubic foot of space that wasn't needed for something else.

"Only in Vegas," he thought with a smile.

Retrieving his suitcase from the luggage carousel, Bud went in search of the shuttle that would take him to his hotel.

# 9

Bud awoke naturally the next morning about twenty minutes before his alarm went off, giving him some extra time to check e-mail and to exchange a few quick 'good morning' text messages with Jane.

Registration at the conference was set to begin officially at 8:00, so Bud had enough time to grab a nice breakfast at one of the hotel's restaurants beforehand. He'd likely be having the conference-provided continental breakfast for the next couple of days, so thought he'd treat himself to a hot meal this morning.

About twelve hundred calories later, Bud wandered past the hotel lobby and through the casino looking for the conference registration area. Ample signs bearing the title 'National Software Development Conference' or 'NSDC' had been provided to point the way, but Bud would not have been surprised to see some sporting the name more commonly applied to the conference, proudly and affectionately, by its devotees: *NerdCon*. Spotting the registration area at last, he got in line at the table marked 'N-Z.'

"Howdy, stranger!" a familiar voice called out.

Bud turned and saw the face he expected, that of Bill Pressman, fellow conference attendee and long-time associate.

"Howdy yourself, Bill," Bud returned.

Mutual smiles and a brief silence followed, after which the two chorused, "We've got to stop meeting like this!"

It was a tradition started so long ago that neither man remembered when it had actually begun. A series of chance encounters at public user group meetings early on in their association had prompted one or the other to say it the first time. It had been their way of greeting each other ever since.

The two shook hands warmly and engaged in small talk as the line inched slowly forward.

"How's it going, Bud? Still over at FiscalWare?"

"Yes, still there after six whole months."

"How's Jane? Well, I hope."

"Jane's fine, thanks. How are Sally and the kids?"

"Everyone's fine, just fine, Bud."

"How's business? Still running your own shop?"

"Yep, still contracting. Don't know how I'd do anything else."

"That's good—really glad to hear that, Bill."

The exchange continued for a while, ending rather abruptly as the two found themselves at the front of the line.

"Name?" asked the volunteer at the registration table.

"Sanders...and Pressman," Bud responded.

The volunteer efficiently located name badges and handed them to the two men, along with conference bags containing about five pounds of printed brochure-like material each, a T-shirt, a conference sessions catalog, a small notebook complete with ball-point pen, and a miniature container of breath mints.

"Welcome to the conference, gentlemen," sang the volunteer. "The opening keynote address begins at 9:00."

Both men acknowledged with smiles and nods, then, as quickly as they could manage with their newly-acquired swag, left the registration area in search of a place to sit.

"Hey, I saw a coffee shop somewhere on the other side of the casino," Bill remarked. "Want to grab a cup and sort through some of this stuff before the keynote?"

"Suits me," Bud answered. "I'll want to dump most of this back in my room, anyway."

This was one of the advantages of staying at the same hotel as the conference. Bud had done it both ways and discovered some time back that he really liked the convenience of having his hotel room nearby.

Bill ordered and fetched the coffee as Bud claimed a table near the entrance. A couple of sips later, both men had their noses in their catalogs, skimming synopses of the sessions that would take place over the next three days.

"I imagine you'll be mostly doing the management track?" Bill speculated.

"Yes, I think so," Bud replied.

Many of the conference sessions were identified as belonging to one of two categories, or 'tracks': *management* or *development*. For the past few years, beginning around the time that Bud's career focus had changed from software development to project management, he had attended mostly management sessions.

"Development track for you, I suppose?" Bud guessed.

"Yep. Some things never change." Bill had been a software developer for his entire working career, and liked it.

"It looks like the keynote is about to begin," said Bud, glancing at his watch. How about we go to that together, then meet up again for lunch after the morning sessions?"

"Love to," Bill concurred. "Do we have enough time to offload some of this stuff?"

"Good idea." Bud smiled. "I'll end up with one arm longer than the other if I lug this around all day. Meet you in the main ballroom."

# 10

Bud joined a line leading into an expansive hall that doubled as a cafeteria during the conference. From where he stood, he could see many such lines, each one leading to its own long table stocked with food and drink. Items on the tables had been arranged so that people could serve themselves from either side.

"Pretty efficient," he thought, as he pondered how he himself would manage the job of feeding roughly three thousand people in a span of ninety minutes. The line was moving at a respectable pace.

Bud pondered the morning's activities as the queue advanced. The keynote address had been fairly interesting, if somewhat stereotypical. The topic had been 'The Future of Software Development,' a much-used title in Bud's experience, but the speaker had been energetic and made some good points about where the industry was heading. Next he had attended a session, one of many listed in the conference catalog, about project management metrics. It seemed that people in management were perpetually coming up with new ways to measure project success.

Plate full, and with drink, utensils and napkin in hand, Bud entered the main seating area and began a slow scan for Bill. Bud eventually spotted him, standing and waving at a table near one corner of the enormous room.

"Howdy, again," Bill offered as Bud approached.

"Howdy, Bill," Bud replied, transferring his bounty to the table. "Long time no see."

"Indeed," Bill chuckled as he arranged his lunch and prepared to dive in. "We didn't get a chance to talk much this morning. Tell me what's been going on with you and FiscalWare. Is Ted Russell still over there?"

"Yes, Ted's still there," Bud replied, recalling that Bill and Ted had also been work associates off and on over the years. Ted had been an independent contractor, like Bill, in the earlier part of his career, and had related many stories to Bud about the projects that he and Bill had worked on together. "In fact," Bud continued, "he still refers to your association as..."

"...'Bill and Ted's Excellent Adventure,'" Bill said, completing the thought. "I'm glad he still feels that way—he was great to work with. Pass my best wishes along to him for me, will you?"

"I certainly will," Bud promised. "And speaking of Ted, he and I were working pretty closely together all last week."

"Really? Going back into development, Bud?" Bill teased, "Or are you trying to entice Ted into the world of management?"

"Neither one, actually. We've got a project coming up—in fact Ted's back there working on it right now—and he and I worked together on estimating how much work it entails. By the way, I agree with you about Ted. I probably wouldn't be here talking to you today if not for his help."

"Sounds like him." Bill nodded. "What was the problem?"

"Well, in a nutshell, my manager came to me and asked me for a 'ballpark' estimate that he 'wasn't going to hold me to,'" Bud replied, wiggling his fingers in the gesture commonly known as 'air quotes.'

"Let me guess," Bill interrupted. "Your estimate got turned into an official schedule."

"Exactly!"

"Well, I guess it's nice to know that some things never change," Bill remarked. "So how did Ted help?"

"Essentially by sharing the grunt work with me. We decomposed all of the code development work into tasks and estimated each one."

"That must have taken a goodly amount of time," Bill observed.

"Yes, the better part of a week, if you include organizational meetings along with the actual task breakdown and estimation time."

"And how closely did your final estimate match your 'ballpark' one?"

"Within about ten percent," Bud answered. "Close enough to make me feel comfortable about taking a week off to be here."

Bud could tell by the look on Bill's face, and by the length of the intervening silence, that he was formulating another question.

"Tell me something," Bill began slowly. "Did you make your estimates in hours?"

"Days, actually," Bud responded. "We didn't feel as if we had enough time to do a finer breakdown. Why do you ask?"

"Just curious, mostly. Are you, by any chance, planning to attend Ethan Green's session tomorrow?"

"I hadn't been," Bud replied, "Who's Ethan Green?"

"Here, give me a minute." Bill dropped knife and fork, fished his conference session catalog out of a backpack, and began to leaf through it. Eventually finding what he was looking for, he handed the catalog to Bud, referring him to a particular spot on the page.

Next to Bill's index finger, Bud saw a synopsis which read:

> **Relative Estimation** - *Don't ask your developers how long something is going to take. They don't know. This hands-on workshop is designed to let you experience a technique for estimating project work that leverages the knowledge and unique abilities of all the members of your development team.*

"Well, that's intriguing," Bud remarked. "Wish I'd been able to attend that session a couple of weeks ago. Are you recommending this?"

"Yeah, I think you'll find it interesting," Bill replied. "I met Ethan last year at another conference. I attended this same workshop when he delivered it there."

Bud consulted his smartphone calendar. He was in the habit of using it to track the sessions he wished to attend. Seeing no conflict, he tapped in enough information to remind him to attend the session.

When he had finished, he looked up to find that Bill seemed to be observing him closely, with a curious smile on his face.

The smile was infectious. "What are you grinning at?" Bud asked.

"Oh, nothing, really," Bill responded. "Just remembering when I took that workshop. I'd go again if I hadn't committed to something else already. You'll have fun."

"I'm certainly in favor of fun. Thanks for the pointer."

"My pleasure," Bill replied. "Now, how about we get some dessert and talk about me for a change?"

"Suits me. I think I saw a huge plate of cookies at the end of one of the serving tables."

# 11

Bud arrived outside the conference room just a few minutes before Ethan's session was to begin. Peeking inside he observed that most of the seats were already taken. The sign on the door read *Relative Estimation—Ethan Green,* so Bud knew he was in the right place.

Stepping inside, Bud found a seat at one of the tables near the front of the room. He exchanged nods and smiles of greeting with the other people at the table as he sat.

Looking around, Bud saw that he had arrived just in time. Every seat at each of the ten or so tables in the room was now occupied, and people were still looking in the door, searching for vacancies.

"Well, what do you say we get started?" boomed a friendly voice from the front of the room.

The buzz of conversation quickly died down as the attendees turned to focus on the source of the utterance.

"Welcome, everyone, and thanks for coming. I'm Ethan Green, and this session is called Relative Estimation. Everyone in the right place?" Ethan's manner seemed genuinely warm and friendly.

Head nods all around confirmed that everyone was indeed where they intended to be.

"Good," Ethan said after a brief pause. "Now if any of you has attended one of my sessions before, you know that I like to dive right in to the exercise portion and debrief as we go. Another thing you should know, if you don't already, is that the last thing I want to do is stand up here and deliver a lecture. I can't think of anything more dull, for me or for you, than to have me drone on, reading bullet points from a slide deck to you. I'm hoping that this session will be very interactive, so if you have

questions, please feel free to ask them as they arise—don't hold
them until the end. That way I believe we'll all get the most out
of the next seventy-five minutes. Sound good?"

Ethan waited as he slowly scanned the room for signs of
agreement. "OK, then," he said at last. "Let's get started."

"Now first let me ask," he went on, "how many of you here
are involved in estimation in some way in the work you do?
That is, does your work require you to either ask for or provide
estimates? Let's see a show of hands."

Bud observed that every hand in the room went up,
including his own.

"OK, good," Ethan continued. "Now let's take another quick
poll—how many of you are on the 'asking for estimates' side of
the equation?"

Bud noted that about half of the people raised their hands.

"OK, that's fine. Now just one more poll," Ethan went on.
"How many of you are called upon to provide estimates in the
work you do?"

Bud was a little surprised to find that all hands in the room
were raised again.

"Yes, that's about what I expected," Ethan explained. "I'd
guess, based on what we've just seen, that even those people
who ask others for estimates in their work are also responsible
for providing estimates to someone 'higher up' in management.
Does that sound about right?"

A combination of head nods and 'thumbs-up' gestures
confirmed general agreement with Ethan's guess.

"We seem to have a lot of experience with estimation in the
room," Ethan forged ahead. "So let me ask you this—why do
you estimate?"

There were a few brief moments of silence, during which
most of the folks present, Bud included, looked around the
room waiting for someone to offer an answer.

Eventually a woman in the back of the room raised her hand
and offered, "for planning?"

"For planning, yes," Ethan responded. "Tell us a little more about what you mean by that."

"Well," the woman continued, "my manager comes to me and asks me to estimate how long my work is going to take so that he can include it in the project plan."

"Good, thanks," Ethan replied. "Anyone else? Why do you estimate?"

"So I can know how much work I should get done each week," said a man at Bud's table.

"That's interesting," Ethan replied. "Are you saying that estimating before doing the work helps keep you on track?"

"Yes, pretty much," the man answered. "It's about setting goals."

"I see," Ethan responded. "Are the goals yours or someone else's?"

"Both, actually. I set goals for myself, and my supervisor also sets goals for me."

"Got it, thanks," Ethan said. "Anyone else? Why do you estimate?"

A young woman in the middle of the room spoke up. "Because my manager tells me to."

The ensuing chuckle offered up by the room at large told Bud that the experience of the young woman was familiar to most of the people there.

"I see by the reaction to your answer that many people here are in that same boat," Ethan suggested with a smile. "Is that right? Are some of you providing estimates without knowing why?"

"I am," volunteered a man at the table next to Bud's. "I'm asked to make estimates all the time, for 'planning purposes' like the lady said earlier—although I don't know how much good they're doing, since we never seem to be able to follow the plan, or I should say 'the schedule.'"

Ethan nodded. "Is that a common experience? Let's see a show of hands."

Bud noted that more than half of the people in the room raised their hands.

"Well, let me ask you this," Ethan continued. "When someone comes to you for an estimate, how do they make that request? What do they say?"

The answer came in chorus, almost as if rehearsed. "'How long is it going to take?'"

This time the laughter was loud enough to be heard in the next room. Bud found himself joining in as he recalled that conversation with Bob Harvey not so long ago.

"Ah," Ethan said, after the sound of amusement had mostly subsided. "Well, here's the thing—A good friend and associate of mine is fond of saying, 'Don't ask your people *how long* something is going to take. They don't know.'"

Bud wasn't sure he agreed with this sentiment, having just gone through several days with several people at FiscalWare doing just that—estimating how long the FutureCash project was going to take.

"Now, mind you, I'm not saying that knowing how long something is going to take is unimportant," Ethan went on. "It's absolutely necessary if we're going to be able to predict schedules—something that's very important in running a business.

"The thing is," he continued, "we human beings generally aren't very good at estimating things in absolute terms. Allow me to demonstrate with a few examples.

"First of all, how tall would you say I am? Any estimates?"

A couple of people had answers.

"Around six feet."

"Between five-foot-nine and six-three."

"I'd say those are reasonable estimates," Ethan responded. "How certain are you?"

The silence that followed was sufficient answer.

"Now let's try that again—for this I'll need a volunteer." He looked at Bud and invited him to the front of the room by eye.

Bud stood beside Ethan, who introduced himself formally and extended his hand. "Ethan Green."

"Bud Sanders," said Bud, accepting the handshake with a grin.

Ethan turned to his audience and asked, "Which of us would you say is taller?"

This time the answer was unanimous. "Bud!"

"So you're certain," Ethan observed. "Thanks for the help, Bud. And now let's try something else.

"How long would it take you to walk from here to the casino downstairs? Any guesses?"

Again there were a few.

"About five minutes."

"Ten minutes."

"Maybe seven or eight minutes."

"And how certain are you?" Ethan asked.

A now familiar silence followed.

"Now let me put that another way," Ethan pressed on. "Which would take longer—walking from here to the casino or from here to your hotel room?"

The room responded with a resounding, "Hotel room!"

"How do you know?" Ethan queried.

A woman in the back answered, "I have to walk *through* the casino to get to my room, therefore walking to my room will take longer."

"Exactly right," Ethan replied. "And my point is, you may not know how long either trip takes—the *absolute* time—but you have a good sense for which is longer—the *relative* time. Same with the height 'competition' I just had with Bud, here. You weren't certain of my *absolute* height, but you knew beyond any doubt that Bud is taller—you correctly gauged our *relative* heights.

"And since we're in Vegas, it occurs to me that there's another example of how we're more adept at employing relative measures over absolute ones. Would you say you've got a better chance of winning at blackjack or at roulette?"

"Blackjack!"

"And why is that?"

A man behind Bud answered, "To win at roulette, I have to guess which number will come up. To win at blackjack, I just have to get a better hand than the dealer."

"Very true," Ethan agreed. "And based on that, would you say that your current estimates at work are more like roulette or like blackjack?"

"Roulette!" was the almost unanimous response.

"Probably right," Ethan said. "And now, before we get to our exercise, let me ask you this—when you provide estimates, what *units* do you use?"

Several people responded.

"Hours."

"Days."

"Man-days."

"So you're providing estimates in *absolute* units, " Ethan remarked. After sensing general agreement from the crowd, he continued, "I'd like to show you a technique for estimating in relative units instead. Are you ready? Good. Allow me to demonstrate."

# 12

Ethan moved to a table at the front of the conference room and picked up a pad of sticky notes from among a collection of various other materials, then turned to face his audience.

"In a few moments," Ethan began, "we're all going to take part in an exercise in relative estimation. Right now I'm going to show you how to play.

"I have in my hand a short stack of cards, similar to ones you'll be getting later. The only difference is that mine are sticky and yours are not. I need to stick these to the whiteboard so that you can all see them, but you'll be using your tabletops to play on.

"You'll be working in teams, so I'll demonstrate this by playing the parts of several team members. Each card represents a chunk of work that needs to be done, and we'll call that chunk of work a *feature*.

"In this game, the first player has the easiest move." Ethan peeled the top sticky note from the pad and held it up so that everyone could see the capital letter A written on it. "As you can see, this card represents *feature A*. Now, as the first player, it's my job to estimate how long it will take to implement *feature A* relative to all the other features on the playing surface," he said as he pointed to the whiteboard behind him. "Since there are no other features on the board yet, I'll just put this somewhere in the middle."

```
┌───┐
│ A │
└───┘
```

"Now it gets a little more interesting," Ethan continued. "As the second player, I take the top card from the deck." He peeled off the top sticky note and held it up so that everyone could see the capital B written there. "Once again, my job is to estimate the time required to implement this feature, relative to the ones already on the playing surface. As the second player, I believe that *feature B* will take less time to implement than *feature A*, so I'll place it to the left, like so."

With that, Ethan placed the B card to the left of the A card on the whiteboard, and added a legend as a reminder of the relative time scale.

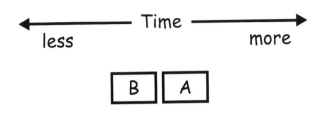

"Now it gets even more interesting," Ethan went on. "From here on, each player has two choices. They can either play the top card off the deck, as we've already seen, or they can change the relative position of one of the cards already on the playing surface. So let's say that, as player 3, I believe that player 2 was wrong, and that *feature B* will actually require more time to implement than *feature A*. I can use my turn to express that, and so I will move the B card to the right of the A card."

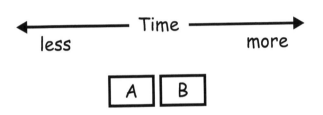

Bud thought he saw a possible conflict here, so he raised his hand and asked, "What if player 2 doesn't agree? Can he move the B card back to the left?"

"Yes, he can," Ethan answered, "but only when it's his turn again. In fact anyone can use his or her turn to disagree with an estimate that's already been made."

"OK, let's see," Ethan continued. "Now I'm player 4, and I believe I'll play off the deck." He peeled the next sticky note from the stack and asked, "Anyone want to guess what the next feature is?"

The whole room shouted, "Feature C!"

"Exactly right," Ethan responded with a smile, adding, "have you played this game before?"

He went on without waiting for an answer. "As player 4, I believe that *feature C* will require roughly the same amount of time to implement as *feature A*, so I'm going to put it in the same column."

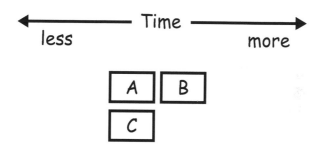

"From this point it's just the same moves over and over again," Ethan said. "Taking turns, you can either play one card from the deck, or change the relative estimate for one card already on the board."

"You may also find," Ethan elaborated, "that in order to get the relative estimates right, you have to clear space for a new column to insert a new card, as I've done with *feature E*."

As he talked, he demonstrated the possible moves, adding a few more cards to the board and rearranging some that were already there.

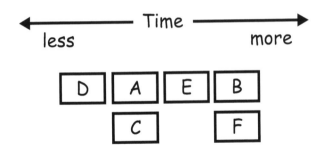

"Is that fairly clear?" Ethan asked. "Does anyone have a question about the process so far?"

A woman at the table next to Bud's raised her hand. "Are we supposed to remain silent as we play, or should we say why we're making the moves we make?"

"Good question," Ethan replied. "I'm in favor of revealing useful information, so I think it's a good idea to state the reasoning behind your moves. Don't bother trying to reach consensus, however. Just use your turn to make your own estimate—if someone disagrees, they can use their turn to express that."

"What about infinite loops?" asked a man near the back of the room.

"Ah, yes," Ethan responded. "I presume that you're asking about what happens if two players keep repositioning the same card over and over again. That may happen—in fact, I've seen it happen many times in presenting this session to lots of people. Trust me, though—these things have a way of resolving themselves, as you may get a chance to see when you play.

"And if there are no more questions," Ethan continued while scanning the room, "let's go ahead with the exercise. You'll be playing in teams so, since we have a capacity crowd here today, let's say that your teammates are the people seated at your own table."

Ethan moved to the table at the front of the room once again, this time picking up many rubber-banded decks of index cards, which he proceeded to hand out, one deck to each table.

"Each team is getting a deck of a dozen cards. Each card bears a particular 'feature' which, in this case is the name of a piece of fruit. Go ahead and spread the cards out on the table in front of you so that you can see them all."

The man across the table from Bud started spreading the cards out, revealing the makings of a what would certainly be a very peculiar kind of fruit salad.

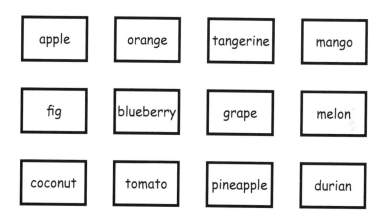

After a brief pause to let everyone examine their 'features,' Ethan continued, "Now please collect all your cards, shuffle them if you like, and place them in a single deck."

When the flurry of activity ceased, Ethan went on. "Now wouldn't you like to know what it is you're supposed to estimate?"

The room was in general agreement.

"Sure."

"That would be nice."

"Yes, I suppose that would help."

"Your job," Ethan continued, "is to estimate the relative time you believe it will take for your team to consume each fruit."

"And by 'consume' you mean 'eat?'" asked a woman near the front of the room.

"Yes, I do," Ethan concurred. "And you may assume that you receive the fruit in roughly the same form as you would find it in your local produce market. In other words, you don't need to climb the tree or shake the vine, or whatever it takes to harvest the fruit. You should estimate only the relative time it will take to prepare and eat it.

"Are there any other questions? No? OK, then. Pick who goes first, remember to take turns, and begin estimating. I'll be walking around looking over your shoulders."

The first player on Bud's team was April, who had no choice but to place the top card by itself on the table.

```
┌─────────────┐
│   tomato    │
└─────────────┘
```

Bud was next and had to play from the deck as well. The top card said *grape*, and its placement was obvious.

```
┌─────────┐ ┌─────────┐
│  grape  │ │ tomato  │
└─────────┘ └─────────┘
```

"Looks like it's my turn," said Chuck. Drawing the top card, *tangerine*, from the deck, he placed it to the right, saying, "it'll take time to peel this, so I think it'll take longer than the tomato."

Next up was Daria, who also chose to play from the deck. "A *blueberry* is kind of a one-bite proposition, like a grape, so I'm going to put it in the same column."

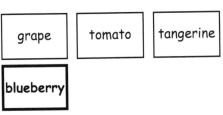

Ed was next, and drew *orange* from the deck. "That seems about the same effort as a tangerine," he declared, "so I'm going to put it in the same column."

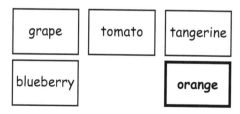

Fiona was the last of the six players, and was of the opinion that an orange was more time-consuming to eat than a tangerine. "A tangerine is both smaller and easier to peel than an orange," she explained, moving *orange* to the right of tangerine.

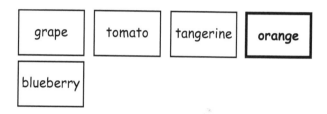

When it was Bud's turn again, he was fairly satisfied with the estimates on the table. He was stymied, though by the card on top of the deck, which read *durian*.

"Anyone have any idea what a durian is?" he asked his teammates. No one at the table had heard of one before, so Bud place it to the right of orange, largely due to his uncertainty.

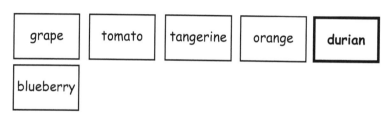

Ethan happened to be looking over Bud's shoulder while this conversation was taking place, and volunteered, "Yes, that's what I would have done, too. This is like receiving specifications that are unclear in a real-world project. It's pretty safe to assume that a feature you don't understand will take a long time to implement, so placing a large estimate on the durian is a reasonable move."

Bud wanted to ask Ethan what a durian was, but by that time he had moved on to another table.

Play proceeded round-robin fashion, each person taking his or her turn to play a new card or move an existing one, until all the cards were out and no one wanted to argue about the estimates any longer.

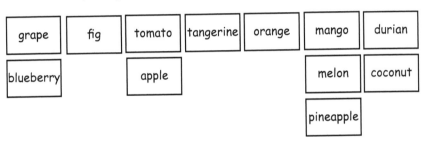

"It looks like most of the teams are finished, "Ethan commented. "Anyone need a little more time? All done? OK, then, let's see where we are.

"First of all, I want to invite everyone to look around and see what estimates the other teams have made." After a brief pause, he continued, "Do the other teams' estimates match your own?"

"No."

"Not really."

"Close, but not exactly."

"And why is that, do you suppose?" Ethan asked.

Bud was the first to offer an explanation. "I'd guess that there are different levels of expertise on the different teams."

"That seems likely," Ethan agreed. "But why does that make a difference?"

"Well, for example," Bud explained, "none of us on this team knew what a durian was, so we estimated a larger relative time to eat it. I overheard people on some of the other teams describing the fruit, so I'd say they had experts where we did not."

"Yes, that would make a difference, "Ethan said. "Anyone else have an idea about why the estimates might differ from team to team?"

A woman at a corner table raised her hand. "We had some wrangling over what kind of tomato it was. Some thought it was something like a beefsteak tomato, while others imagined a cherry tomato."

"And what did you decide?" Ethan asked.

"We ended up calling it a beefsteak tomato, so we estimated it larger," the woman replied.

"So you made an assumption. Do you ever have occasion to do that when estimating your real work?"

"Yes, all the time. Sometimes we don't have clear specifications, so we make a guess. Personally I tend to assume the worst case, so I tend to estimate higher if I'm uncertain."

"Fair enough," Ethan replied. "Now let me ask you all another question. Since the main purpose of estimation is to provide predictable schedules, do you have enough information in front of you at this point for that? In other words, can you tell me how long it's going to take to eat all this fruit?"

"No."

"We could guess."

"Not really."

"Sounds like the answer is 'no,'" Ethan concluded. "Tell me why."

"No numbers," a man at the back volunteered.

"Right you are," Ethan replied. "To expand on that, so far all we've done is to say what's bigger than what. To get even close to predicting how long it will take to eat the fruit, we'll have to quantify the results. In other words, we need to know *how much more* time one fruit will take to eat compared to another. And if you're ready for that, we'll start phase two of the exercise."

Ethan moved again to the table of materials and picked up another pad of sticky notes and another collection of rubber-banded decks of index cards. He divided the index cards into two parts and handed them to people at the two tables nearest him.

"If you'll get these passed out to the room," he requested, "I'll go ahead and explain how we're going to quantify our estimates."

Ethan walked to the whiteboard as the index cards were handed out, one deck per table. Raising the pad of sticky notes in the air, he began, "I have in my hand a set of cards, much like the ones you're receiving now, except, again, that mine are sticky. As soon as you get your cards, please lay them out on the table so that you can see what's printed on them."

Bud's teammates had already begun arranging the cards so that they could see them all.

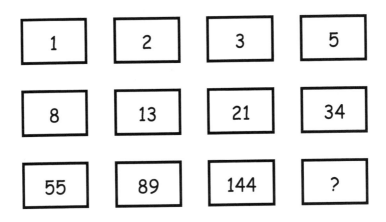

Ethan waited until the cards at every table were visible, then went on. "You can see that each card has a different number printed on it," he said. "Does anyone recognize this particular sequence of numbers?"

"Those are the Fibonacci numbers," said a man in the middle of the room.

"Exactly right," Ethan replied. "Care to tell the group about them?"

"Sure," the man continued. "To create the Fibonacci sequence, you add two numbers to get the next number in the sequence. In other words, one plus two gives you three. Two plus three gives you five. Three plus five gives you eight, and so on."

"And why are they called 'Fibonacci' numbers?"

"Named for the inventor, I believe. An Italian mathematician from a long time ago."

"Right again," Ethan confirmed. "And there's a notable characteristic of these numbers that makes them useful for estimating, namely that as the numbers grow larger, so do the gaps between them. The size of the gaps can be used to represent the amount of uncertainty there is in an estimate.

"Another way to say this," Ethan continued, "is that the larger an estimate is, the less precise it is likely to be. Using the Fibonacci numbers to estimate helps prevent us from believing that our estimates have precision that's not really there. The number system itself prevents us from wrangling and agonizing over estimating whether a feature is, say, a 20 or a 21 or a 22. Our only choice is to pick one of the available numbers, and that saves a lot of time and effort."

"But what's a 21?" Bud asked. "Are these in units of days or hours, or what?"

"Glad you asked," Ethan replied. "You can consider these to be unitless. In other words, they're not directly related to any real-world clock or calendar time. We typically just refer to them as 'points.'

"Their only purpose," he went on, "is to quantify the relative time required to implement different features. For example, a 2 represents twice as much time as a 1. Likewise, a 3 represents one-and-a-half times as much time as a 2, and so on.

"And if there are no more questions about the number system, I'd like to move on and demonstrate how to play this phase of the game. Sound good?"

Turning to the whiteboard again, Ethan pointed to the 'feature' cards he had placed there previously.

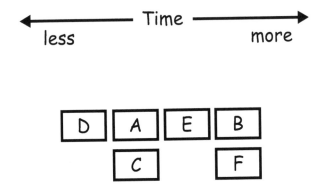

"In this part of the game," he began, "you're going to take turns again, just as you did before. But now, instead of ordering the features by relative time, you're going to use your turn to estimate what's already there by placing a number card at the top of a column.

"There are different ways to proceed, but an easy way to get started is for the first player—that's me—to decide whether the leftmost feature, *feature D* in this case, represents the smallest feature we will ever have to estimate. If it is, then I simply put the *1* there."

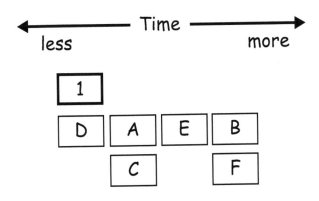

"Now, as the second player, I want to place a number at the top of one of the other columns that reflects *how much more* time I believe it will take to implement each of the features in that column, relative to what's there already. In this case, I believe that any feature in the second column will take roughly three times as long to implement as feature D, so I'll put a *3* there."

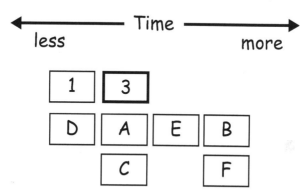

"And as the third player," Ethan continued, "I believe that *feature E* in the third column will take roughly one-and-a-half times to implement as anything in the second column. Since I don't have a card that says 4½, I'll pick the closest one and put a *5* there."

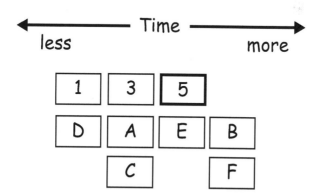

"So far, so good," Ethan went on, "but as the fourth player I'm going to introduce a little wrinkle. I think that player three has underestimated *feature E*, so I'm going to bump it up by placing the *8* there instead.

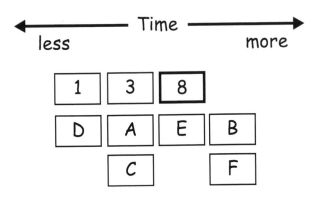

"Now, as the fifth player, I also have a problem with what's on the board. I want to estimate *features B and F* in the fourth column, but the next number available to me is a 13. I believe that features B and F are closer to an *8* than they are to a *13*, so I'm going to move them both into the third column to reflect that."

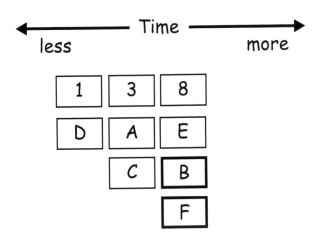

"Finally, as the sixth player, I also want to change the board a little. I think that feature B will take less time to implement than either of features E or F, but more time than feature A or C. Therefore, I'm going to create a new column, place *feature B* in it, and put a *5* there."

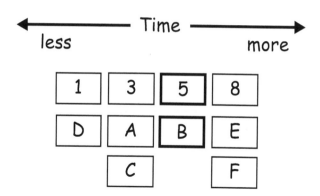

"And those are the basic moves," Ethan said, turning to face the audience. "You can put a number card at the top of a column. You can exchange an existing number card for a new one. You can combine columns, and you can create new columns."

"Do we have to use all the numbers?" Bud asked.

"No, you don't," Ethan replied. "What you're trying to do here is to establish a consistent scale, from far left to far right, that best represents the relative time you think it will take to implement every feature. You should keep adjusting the numbers and columns until you get the best fit.

"One hard and fast rule is, every column has to end up with a number at the top. Another is that the numbers should be in ascending numerical order from left to right."

"For example," Bud volunteered, "One, three, two is a no-no."

"That's right, "Ethan agreed. "Now, are there any more questions about the process?"

"Just one more," Bud stated. "What's the question mark for?"

"Oh, yes," Ethan replied. "That's the 'I dunno' number. You can use that to identify features that you're unable to estimate."

Seeing no more hands raised, Ethan continued, "OK, good. Remember to take turns. Ready, set, estimate!"

Bud's teammates got busy estimating. April went first. "I can't imagine anything that would take less time than eating a blueberry or grape," she said, "so I'm going to put the *1* there."

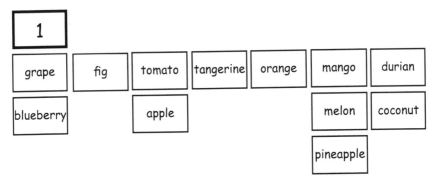

Bud was next, and estimated the fig at *2*.

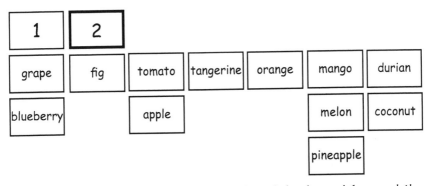

Chuck was next in line. He pondered the board for a while, saying, "I can't decide whether the tomato and apple should be a 3 or a 5. We have a fig tree behind our house, but I never paid much attention to the fruit on it. Do you just pull those off the tree and eat them, or is there some kind of preparation?"

"No, you can just wash and eat them whole," Daria replied.

"OK, thanks. In that case, since tomato and apple require considerably more prep, I'm going to estimate them at *5*."

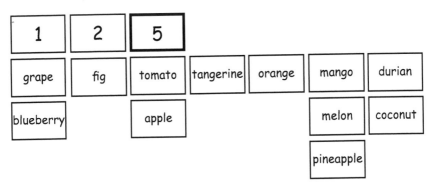

Now it was Daria's turn. She studied the board for a few moments. "It seems to me that the time to consume a tangerine is so close to that of a tomato or apple," she said, "that I'm going to move it into the same column with them."

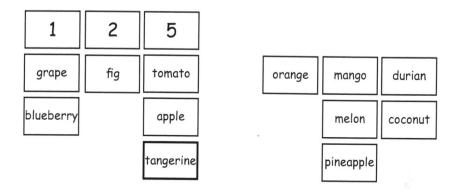

"What about orange, then," April asked. Do you want to move that, too?"

"I'm not sure," Daria replied. "Anyway, I think that would require another turn, if I understand the rules correctly."

Daria's opinion was confirmed as she looked up to see Ethan giving her the thumbs-up gesture.

Ed was up next. In an unprecedented move, he placed the *144* above the column with the durian. "Don't know if this is legal, or if I'm supposed to work from left to right," he said. "That pesky durian has been bothering me, so I wanted to put a large number on it. That might help establish the scale."

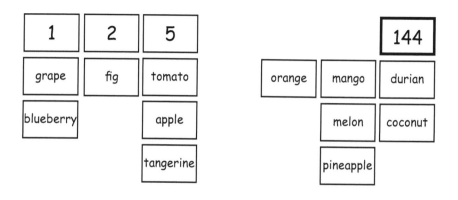

"Maybe we can get a ruling from Ethan on this," Bud said, waving his hand to get Ethan's attention. When he arrived, Bud said, pointing to the table, "This 144 was the last move made. Is that legal, or are we supposed to work in order?"

"That seems fine to me," Ethan replied. "The important thing is that you end up with numbers above every column. You don't need to work from left to right if you don't want to."

"OK, thanks," Bud said. "Fiona, I guess it's your turn next."

"Yep, and I'm going to work my way back from the right," she said, placing the *89* above mango, melon and pineapple.

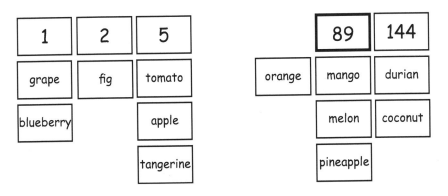

The team having played around the circle once, it was April's turn again. She decided to move *orange* into the same column as tangerine.

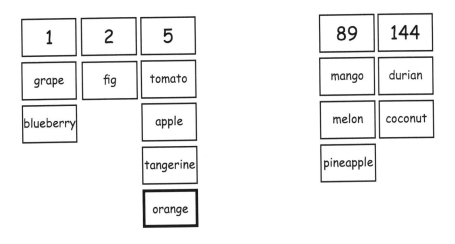

Play continued around the circle without too much wrangling and only the merest of friendly arguments. Within about 15 minutes, Bud's team arrived at a set of estimates they could all agree on.

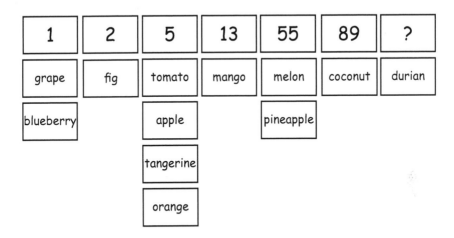

| 1 | 2 | 5 | 13 | 55 | 89 | ? |
|---|---|---|---|---|---|---|
| grape | fig | tomato | mango | melon | coconut | durian |
| blueberry | | apple | | pineapple | | |
| | | tangerine | | | | |
| | | orange | | | | |

They finished at about the same time as most of the other teams, so they didn't have to wait long before Ethan declared, "OK, it looks like most, if not all, of the teams are finished, so let's move on.

"At this point I want to ask you the same question I asked at the end of round one. Can you tell me, given the information before you, how long it's going to take for your team to eat all this fruit?"

"Nope."

"I don't think so."

"Not yet."

"Why not? We said we needed numbers, and now we've got numbers."

"Well, the numbers are in relative units," Bud ventured. "There's no way I could go to my manager with an estimate of something like 513 'points' and have him accept that. He's going to want the estimate in absolute units of hours or days."

"Yes, you're probably right," Ethan agreed. "So how do we get from here to there?"

"How about a pilot project?" suggested a woman in the middle of the room.

"That sounds promising," Ethan encouraged. "What do you mean by 'pilot?'"

"Well," the woman responded, "We could time how long it takes to eat, say, a grape, then multiply that by the number of points estimated for all the remaining fruit."

"You're on track," Ethan said enthusiastically. "I can imagine quite a margin for error in that approach, though. Can anyone tell me why?"

Bud ventured a guess. "Probably," he said, "because we're not sure if we can consume everything else at the same rate at which we consume grapes. It would help if we had an idea of the rate at which we could consume a sampling of various fruits, not just grapes."

"Yes, I agree," Ethan said. "But the general idea is the same. What you're both talking about has to do with determining the rate at which we can get work done, that work being eating fruit in this case. Rates are expressed in some units per some period of time, such as miles per hour. For us, a reasonable such expression might be *points per hour*. And we have a special name for this in project work, by the way. We call the rate at which we get work done our *velocity*.

"So if we can get some idea of our velocity, we can begin to predict how long our project is going to take. And in order to get a handle on our velocity, we're going to have to *eat some fruit*.

"Can anyone give me an example, "Ethan continued, "of what 'eating some fruit' corresponds to in the real world of work?"

"Writing some code."

"Creating specifications."

"Product testing."

"Yes, yes and yes," Ethan replied. "The velocity for any person or team can be found by actually doing some work and measuring how long it took. With a velocity figure in hand, plus a set of estimates in relative units, we can project completion dates using basic arithmetic.

"For example, lets say we've estimated that our project contains 500 points, and that our velocity is 50 points per week. How many weeks will it take to get the project done?"

"Ten weeks!" the room responded in chorus.

"Right," Ethan replied, glancing at the clock on the wall. "And speaking of project completion," he said, "I notice that we're just about out of time. That went quickly!

"Just so you know, I'm happy to answer any questions you have. I imagine there's another session in this room in about fifteen minutes, so if you have any questions I'll be right outside in the hallway for as long as I'm needed.

"And with that, let me say thanks for coming, and thanks for playing Relative Estimation!"

A careful observer would have seen Ethan's face grow slightly pinker with the round of enthusiastic applause that followed.

# 13

Bud joined a medium-sized line of people waiting to speak with Ethan by the conference room door. Conference attendees sailed past, seeking their next destinations in the fifteen minute break between sessions, and Bud was glad he hadn't planned to be somewhere else. It looked like it might take a while to get to the front of the line.

But the line dwindled in size quickly enough, and soon he and Ethan were face to face again.

"Well, hello," Ethan said. "Thanks for helping me out before."

"Oh, you're quite welcome," Bud replied, extending his hand. "Happy to do it. I just wanted to say thanks for the great session. I really enjoyed it. Wish there were more of these interactive things at these conferences."

Ethan returned the handshake heartily. "Oh, good—glad to hear that. I really enjoy doing these. They're always a lot of fun."

"I came to your session on a recommendation from a friend of mine—Bill Pressman. He told me he attended this same presentation at a conference sometime last year."

"Can't say the name is familiar, but I do a fair number of these and I'm not especially good at remembering names, although I try," Ethan admitted. "You say he recommended this session?"

"Yes, we were talking yesterday about some estimation I did recently, and he suggested I attend your workshop. Glad he did. I wondered at the time why he asked me if I estimated in hours—now I know."

"If you don't mind my asking, how did your estimation work out?"

"Well, it took a little while, but we got it done," Bud said. Our detailed estimate came within about ten percent of a 'ballpark' I had given earlier, so I felt pretty good about that."

"I see. That sounds *very* recent. You haven't done the work yet, then?"

"No, no," Bud replied. "At least, not much of it. The folks at my company started the project a couple of weeks before I came to the conference, so by the time I get back they'll only have about three weeks of work done."

"How long is the project supposed to take all together?" Ethan asked.

"About three months." Bud experienced a mild feeling of déjà vu, realizing that he had spoken these very same words to Bob Harvey not so long ago in answer to the same question.

"Ah, then it's early yet," Ethan remarked. "Well, I wish you good luck with that. Do you happen to have a business card on you?"

"Yes, I do," Bud replied. Fishing in his backpack, he pulled out a card and handed it to Ethan.

"Thanks, and here's mine," Ethan said. "Please feel free to contact me if you have any questions about this estimation stuff. I'm happy to talk about it any chance I get."

"I appreciate that," Bud said. "And thanks again."

"My pleasure."

Ethan spun on his heels and moved off at a brisk pace.

Bud pondered his own destination for a moment, then headed down the hall that would take him through the casino and back to his room. The idea of a nap was suddenly very appealing, and he vaguely wondered what could have made him so tired.

# 14

Bud had arranged a late-morning flight in order to avoid having to get up too early the day after the conference.

He generally liked to get to the airport about ninety minutes before departure time. Consulting the hotel's shuttle schedule, he found that buses to the airport left every half hour. A quick deliberation led him to opt for arriving twenty minutes early, rather than ten minutes late.

Bud mused for a few moments over past air travel experiences, trying to remember when was the last time he had run through an airport to catch a flight. He smiled at a dim memory of watching the aircraft he was supposed to be on push back from the gate while he stood there, panting from the effort of jogging through the concourse.

The shuttle left the hotel on time, but encountered dense traffic on the freeway. By the time Bud had collected his bag and tipped the driver, his twenty minute excess had shrunk to five.

Bud found his way to the ticketing area and located an available self check-in terminal. He spent a few minutes there before collecting his boarding pass and strolling to the baggage drop-off. Relieved of his rolling burden, he scanned a few overhead signs before spotting one that pointed the way to security.

The queue at security wasn't especially long when he first spotted it, but a lot of other people were apparently heading there, too. By the time he arrived, Bud found himself at the end of a line of about thirty or forty fellow travelers.

Within a few seconds, a gentleman with a medium-sized carry-on bag joined the queue.

Bud waited a few beats before turning to address the man. "What is it," he asked, smiling, "about being at the end of a long line that makes me feel better when someone gets into it behind me?"

The man smiled politely, but obviously didn't find the query as amusing as Bud did. It was one of Bud's standard conversation starters, although this time it fell a little flat.

The queue didn't seem to be moving much. Turning to face the front again, Bud peered toward the head of the line to see if he could spot the reason for the slow progress. From where he stood, he could see past the line he was in to the familiar array of metal tables, rollers and scanners, which seemed mostly unoccupied at the moment. Tracing the path backward from there, his eyes landed on the source of the holdup—a podium at which stood a solitary security official, checking IDs and boarding passes.

In the meantime, Bud's queue grew ever longer as more and more people joined it, while forward progress was slow. Having nothing better to do, Bud watched the activities at the podium, eventually deciding that the screener was letting people through at the rate of about one every 20 seconds.

Unable to help himself, Bud started calculating. "Let's see," he thought, "we've got about 3 people passing through every minute, and there are at least 30 people ahead of me. That means it'll be at least 10 minutes before I get through."

"Ah, well," he added, "it could be worse. I could be at the *end* of this line."

● ● ● ● ●

Bud's plane left the gate on time, and there were no unanticipated delays. The flight was uneventful and, shortly after the aircraft touched down at SFO, Bud sent a text message to Jane, saying that he had arrived safely and would be home in a couple of hours.

# 15

Bud arrived at work Monday morning, refreshed after a pleasant, relaxing weekend. The conference had been fun, but tiring, and it had been nice to loaf for a couple of days before returning to the job.

It was mid-morning when Ted Russell dropped by. "Hey, Bud," Ted said cheerfully. "How was the conference?"

"Hey, yourself, Ted," Bud returned. "The conference was good. Saw a lot of old friends. Bill Pressman sends his regards, by the way."

"Yeah, I wondered if Bill would be there. Is he doing well?"

"He seemed quite happy. He's still in the contracting game, and appears to like it as much as ever."

"That's great," Ted said in earnest. "Bill's a good guy."

"How are things going around here?" Bud asked.

"Same as ever—you know."

Bud felt the need to be a little more specific. "How's the FutureCash project going? Are we on track?"

"Everyone's working really hard on it," Ted replied.

"What I mean is, are we meeting the schedule so far?"

"Well, I think we may have slipped the schedule a little," Ted replied, "but, you know, it's still early. We're only three weeks in—plenty of time to catch back up."

"OK. Any idea how much of a schedule slip we're talking about here?"

"Well," Ted answered slowly, "I'd guess we're probably no more than a week behind. There were some unexpected delays."

"Like what, for example?"

"Oh, for instance, Marj was called on to do some user interface work on another project, so she wasn't able to turn her designs over to us in development until a little later than she had planned."

"I see," Bud replied. "Anything else?"

"Yeah, well, some of the development work we're doing is going to take a little longer than we originally estimated. We did some prototyping with that third-party graphics software—you know, the library that's supposed to display the FutureCash graphs—and it's turned out to be kind of tricky to get the graphs to look like the ones that Marj's group designed."

"None of that sounds too bad," Bud remarked. "Haven't seen a project yet that didn't have some wrinkles. Is that about it?"

"As far as I know, yes," Ted answered. "But I've been fairly busy with the development work. You'd do better asking the various department heads how things are going for them."

"My thoughts exactly." Bud started composing the meeting invitation email in his head, before Ted even left the room.

"Well, I guess I'll let you get to it," Ted said.

"Thanks, Ted. Check your inbox in about fifteen minutes, will you?"

"Yeah, I was planning to." Ted smiled. "Nice to have you back, Bud."

"Thanks. It's good to be back."

As he typed the invitation email, Bud privately toyed with the idea of writing a program that would invite all the departments heads to a status meeting with a single button click. It seemed like he sent one of those out fairly often, and he idly wondered how much time such an application would save him in the course of a year.

# 16

People were just beginning to file in to the conference room when Bud arrived. He had sent out the invitations on Monday morning, but Wednesday afternoon was the first free time slot that all of the department heads had in common.

Karl was the last to arrive this time, about five minutes after the scheduled start.

Noting that all were now present, Bud began. "Hi everyone, and thanks for coming."

This was the first in-person encounter between Bud and most of the department heads since he had returned from his trip.

"Hey, Bud."

"Welcome back!"

"How were things in 'Lost Wages?'"

"Thanks, and things were fine. It was a good conference," Bud replied.

"And now, what do you say we get right to it? I scheduled this meeting for just half an hour because I know everyone is very busy."

Sensing no disagreement, he continued. "I called everyone here just to check in about the status of the FutureCash project. I spoke with Ted a couple of days ago, and he indicated that he thinks development is about a week behind schedule. I'm wondering how things are going in the other departments."

No one spoke up immediately. The various department heads looked at each other as if they hoped someone else would speak first.

Bud scanned the room, looking from person to person for a sign that one of them might have something to say. Eventually, seeing no obvious volunteers, Bud looked at Marj, raising his eyebrows slightly. "Marj? How are things going in user interface design?"

Marj hesitated for a few moments before replying. "Well, things have been crazy for the last week or so. I know that I'm behind on this project, but while you were gone I was pulled off onto another project—Bob Harvey said it was more important. I've been putting in some overtime on FutureCash so that I can try to catch up, but...."

Bud held up his hand before Marj could go on. "I apologize, Marj. Believe me, it wasn't my intention to put you on the defensive. I know you're working hard—I think everyone knows that. I'm really just trying to get a factual assessment of how things are going. No one is getting blamed here." His smile emphasized his point.

"OK, thanks, Bud," Marj said, a little slower this time. "I guess I'm a little frazzled."

"No worries. I gather that, like Ted, you believe you're a little behind schedule."

"Yes, I'd say so," Marj replied.

"Any idea by how much?"

Marj's eyes turned skyward as she pondered the question. "Not sure—I'd guess roughly a week."

"OK, thanks. Anyone else? Are you on schedule, ahead, or behind?"

"When is anyone ever ahead of schedule?" Ted asked, prompting a nervous chuckle from the others in the room.

"Just thought I'd ask," Bud responded. "Anyone care to report?"

"I can't say yet one way or the other," George volunteered. "At this point we're doing some testing, but we won't be getting the bulk of the work from development for another couple of weeks."

"Fair enough," Bud replied. "Who's next?"

"I'd say the database work is on track," Karl offered. "I've been working independently, and I'm just about where I expected to be by this time."

"OK, thanks, Karl," Bud said. "Carol, I guess that leaves just you. How's the documentation coming?"

"Well," Carol replied, "I'm in much the same boat as George. I've been able to do a little documentation so far, but the bulk of the work is yet to come, as development finishes more parts of the application."

"OK, that makes sense," Bud replied, reflecting for a few moments before continuing. "What I think I'm hearing is that, as far as we know, the project is either on track or slightly behind schedule. Is that a fair assessment?"

Bud took some time to note the nods of agreement that followed. "That's what I wanted to find out," he went on. "Does anyone feel at this point that the schedule slip is permanent? Or to put that the other way, is there still a possibility that we'll be able to get back on schedule?"

The response was quite enthusiastic.

"I think so."

"Don't see why not."

"Maybe we'll catch a break on some of the upcoming work."

"OK, then," Bud continued. "Thanks again for coming, everyone. I appreciate it. And let me know if there's anything I can do to help out."

Bud waited until everyone had left the room. The meeting had ended a few minutes early, giving him time to sit and contemplate what had just occurred. It was a familiar position to be in—behind and optimistic. In hindsight, it seemed that almost every project he had ever been on had included this unofficial phase.

Pausing only to turn off the room lights, Bud strolled back to his office, wondering what his next move would be.

# 17

Traffic on the drive home was noticeably more congested than normal. Bud had left work a little early, intending to mull over what he had heard in the status meeting, but the slow-and-go traffic occupied most of his attention at the moment.

As he drove, he observed a familiar pattern. He would drive along for a while, moving at a speed considerably less than the limit, but moving. Brake lights ahead of him would come on, he would hit the brake and slow down—sometimes stop. Cars ahead would then begin to speed up again—not all at once, but one after the other, taking turns. Eventually a gap would open up between his car and the one immediately in front, and Bud would accelerate until he was moving again, still slower than the speed limit. Then the whole cycle would repeat.

"Seems like we could do better than this," he mumbled. Bud was only occasionally aware of speaking his thoughts aloud when driving alone.

Eventually, and in the span of just a few minutes, the congestion cleared. It was as if half of the cars had suddenly left the freeway. But there had been no major exits or intersections in the past few miles, nor had the number of lanes increased.

"Another of life's mysteries," Bud muttered, shaking his head.

Exiting the freeway relaxed him some, and the trend continued as he pulled into his driveway a few minutes later. He grinned as usual upon hearing the familiar greeting that welcomed him.

"Honey, you're home!" Jane sang out.

"Indeed, and glad to be here," he returned. They exchanged a hug and a kiss, as was their custom.

"Rough day at the office, dear?" she asked. Their after-work greeting ritual tended to sound a lot like the dialogue found in television shows from the 1950s, of which they were both fans.

"No more than usual," Bud replied automatically, then changed his response. "Well, a little more than usual, I guess."

Jane started to really pay attention. "I was just making dinner. Want to come in and tell me about it?"

Bud followed Jane through the house and took a seat at the counter that bordered the kitchen. Jane busied herself with cutting and chopping while she waited for Bud to settle in, knowing that he would talk when he was ready.

"It's nothing major, really," he began. "We had that status meeting this afternoon—you know, about the FutureCash project."

Jane nodded, silently encouraging him to continue.

"You remember, I told you a couple of days ago that Ted Russell thought development was about a week behind schedule. Today's meeting tended to confirm that—half of the department heads feel like they're at least a little behind."

Jane listened patiently, sensing that he was just getting started.

"No one seemed defeated, or anything like that," he went on. "To the contrary, the general tone of the meeting was one of optimism—they all feel like we can get back on schedule. The thing is, people were working hard before I left for the conference, and they're still working hard. In fact, Marj is already putting in overtime in order to catch up."

Bud paused in thought before continuing. "I guess what I'm wondering is, where is this optimism coming from? From a certain perspective, it seems like just so much wishful thinking. I certainly can't see any factual basis for it.

"And it's all a little too familiar. Since I started in management, and even before then, really, I've seen this kind of thing on almost every project I've been on. We make estimates, they don't pan out, and then we work harder, hoping to catch up. But we almost never do.

"I guess what I'm saying is, I'd rather not go through this cycle again if I can avoid it. It would be nice to deliver on time for a change."

Inferring that he hadn't yet revealed the entire situation, Jane decided to save the questions that were popping up in her head for a bit longer.

"And now that I think about it," Bud went on, "there's something else that's bothering me about this—two things, in fact. First, why do we believe that there's a way that we can actually catch up? Experience doesn't show it. If I look back over all of my project work, both at FiscalWare and elsewhere, that scenario has only occurred on the rare occasion. Mostly what happens is, once we fall behind we stay behind."

After a long silence, Jane prompted, "You mentioned a second thing?"

Bud returned from his musings. "Oh, yes. The second thing is, how do we know we're actually behind at all?"

Jane's curiosity overrode her earlier decision to refrain from asking questions. "What do you mean?"

"I mean, what facts do we have to indicate that we're behind schedule? When I think about it, I realize that all we're going on, at least so far, are feelings that people have. Ted said he *felt* like we're about a week behind. Marj *guessed* at about the same figure. And if I'm honest about it, I've got to admit that I'm basing my assessment mostly on my observation that people are starting to put in some overtime."

"Isn't *that* a fact, that they're putting in overtime?" Jane prompted.

"Yes, I suppose so," Bud answered, "but I suspect that they're only working more because they feel they're behind, so it's a fact, or rather a behavior, based on feelings. It's a shaky foundation."

"Sounds to me like you've uncovered the main issue," Jane ventured. "I'd say the situation you're facing is that you don't know where you are in relation to the schedule because you don't have any real facts about it. Is that right?"

"Yes, I believe it is," Bud replied.

"I can't help but wonder, then," Jane continued, "what kind of facts you're talking about here. In other words, what facts would you need to let you know where you are, schedule-wise?"

"Good question." Bud mulled this over for a while before answering. "It's pretty straightforward, really. I would need to know the rate at which we're getting work done. I already know the project deadline. Given those two facts, I should be able to say if we're on schedule or behind. Or ahead."

"That sounds simple enough," Jane said, "but don't you know both of those things already?"

"Seems like I should but, no, I don't believe so."

Jane was definitely intrigued now. "Do tell," she prompted.

Bud was starting to enjoy this. "Well, If I think about it, I'm inclined to believe that people's *feelings* about being behind schedule actually do have some rational basis. And the only basis I can imagine, at least right now, is that tasks are taking longer to complete than expected."

"Tasks are taking longer to complete than expected," Jane echoed. "Isn't that another fact?"

"Well, maybe. It certainly seems like a fact, but I'm a little suspicious of it, so I'm going to call it a *factoid*. What I mean is, is it reasonable to say we're behind schedule just because tasks are taking longer than expected?"

"Isn't it?" Jane was puzzled.

"Let me see if I can get at this another way," Bud said. "When I was driving home today, I found myself in a traffic jam. Traffic was slow-and-go, and the average speed of the traffic was substantially less than the limit. Now let's say, just to make the arithmetic easy, that the distance from work to home is exactly 60 miles, and that the speed limit is 60 miles per hour. My expectation, starting out, would be to arrive home in 1 hour. Right?"

"So far, so good," Jane replied.

"And when I found myself in the traffic jam, travelling at less than the limit, I knew that my 'task'—driving home—would take longer than expected to complete."

"Yes, I see," Jane said.

"Therefore, I concluded that I was 'behind schedule.'"

"Seems completely reasonable, but I'm not sure I see your point."

"My point is," Bud went on, "that when I'm driving I have the essential facts in hand—I know the expected completion time, and I know what velocity I need to maintain in order to arrive at that time. Any slower than that, and I know I'm behind schedule."

"Yes, I get that," Jane replied. "But what about catching up?"

"Ah, yes, there's the other point. Let's have a look." Bud paused while he considered how to express it. "Just to keep it simple, let's say that, rather than a delay on the road, I delay my start instead."

"OK."

"Let's further say," he continued, "that the delay is 30 minutes long. That will definitely put me behind schedule."

"Definitely."

"The question becomes, what velocity would I have to maintain in order to 'catch up'—meaning arrive home at the expected time?"

"Given those figures, 120 miles per hour," Jane answered.

"Yep. Am I actually going to be able to do that?"

"Not if the highway patrol has anything to say about it."

"That's right, Bud said. "If we assume that I'm not allowed to break the speed limit, then catching up is not an option."

"Oh, right," Jane said. "So, likewise, if there's some kind of 'speed limit' on your project, then there's no way to catch up once you fall behind."

"That's what I'm saying," Bud concurred.

"Well, then, can't you just apply the same principles to your project? You already said you know the project deadline, right?"

Yes, that's true," Bud responded.

"So it seems that all you need to know is your velocity," Jane said, then added, "and perhaps your 'speed limit,' if there is such a thing."

"Yes, that's how it seems," Bud agreed.

"Well, I have to ask," Jane went on. "Why don't you know your velocity?"

At times like this, Jane claimed that she could hear the buzz-whirr-click emitted by the gears in Bud's head as he tried to puzzle out an answer.

"God, I'm an idiot!" Bud exclaimed.

"You can't talk about my husband that way!" Jane responded automatically. Eventually she continued. "Why are you an idiot?"

"Do you remember the estimation session I told you about— the one at the conference?"

"Yes, I do. Ethan somebody, right?"

"Yeah, Ethan Green. The focus was on velocity and estimating in relative time."

"OK. Why are you an idiot?"

"Because it took me this long to realize that what he was talking about might apply to my project. I was so engaged in the exercise, I apparently just glossed over the idea that it might actually be relevant.

"We don't have any straightforward way of expressing velocity on our project." Bud went on. Therefore, we really can't know where we are in relation to the schedule. Plus, we're estimating in absolute units, not relative ones."

"Is that a requirement?" Jane asked.

"I'm not entirely sure yet, but I know how to find out." He leapt from his chair and went in search of the backpack that held the business cards he'd collected at the conference.

"Dinner in five minutes!" Jane called after him, pleased to see that his earlier sense of frustration had been transformed into a call for action. That was progress.

# 18

Bud sat in his office at work on Friday morning, eagerly anticipating the upcoming call with Ethan Green. He had sent an email to Ethan the previous morning, requesting a phone call that he hoped would take place that same day. Ethan's response had been cordial, and Bud was pleased to learn that Ethan had some free time today.

The phone sounded on the dot, and Bud answered on the second ring. "Hi, this is Bud."

"Hi, Bud. Ethan Green."

"Hi, Ethan. Thanks for calling. How are you?"

"Fine, thanks. How about you?"

"I'm good. Not sure if you remember me from the NSDC conference—I was in your estimation session and..."

"You're the guy who's obviously taller than me," Ethan broke in.

"That's right. We talked in the hall afterwards."

"Yes, I remember."

A brief pause ensued while both men waited to find out who was going to take the lead. It was Bud who finally broke the silence.

"I don't want to take up too much of your time. Like it said in the email I sent you, I'm trying to find out if there's a way we can determine if our project is on schedule or not."

"Happy to help if I can," Ethan said.

"OK, great! How about if I tell you a little about what we're doing, first?"

"Sounds fine. Understanding the context certainly can't hurt."

"Good," Bud continued. "Well, as I said, I'm overseeing a project at FiscalWare. We're adding a new feature called FutureCash to our MoneyMap product.

"We started work on the project before the conference so, as of today, we're four weeks in. The total project duration is supposed to be about fourteen weeks."

"And you're trying to assess whether you're on track, is that right?"

"Yes, that's it."

"Sounds pretty straightforward," Ethan remarked. "Mind if I ask you a few questions to help fill in the picture a little?"

"Please do," Bud replied.

"Good. First thing that comes to mind is, do you have a pretty clear idea about how much total work there is in the project, and how that breaks down?"

"Well," Bud answered, "we have a detailed requirements document, and we did a pretty thorough task breakdown prior to beginning the work, so I'd say yes—I think we understand the nature and volume of what needs to get done."

"That's good to know. I seem to recall you mentioning doing some estimation prior to the start of the project."

Bud was impressed. He had mentioned that fact to Ethan while at the conference, but not since, and hadn't expected him to remember it. "Yes, we did."

"And am I correct in assuming that you estimated each one of those tasks?"

"Yes, that's right," Bud replied. "Well, not me personally— The task breakdowns and estimates were done by people in each department."

"Ah, OK. How many departments?"

"Well, there's user interface design, software development, testing, database design and documentation, so five," Bud declared.

"And each department estimated its own work?"

"Yes. It seemed the best way to go about it."

"I tend to agree with that," Ethan concurred. "And in what units did you make your estimates?"

"I knew you were going to ask me that!" Bud exclaimed. "Just so you know, I had never even heard of estimating in 'points' until I attended your session."

Ethan chuckled. "Not to worry, Bud. It wasn't so long ago that I hadn't heard of estimating in points, either. So your estimates were in..."

"Days," Bud replied. "I considered using hours instead, but it seemed that estimating to that level of detail might take too long."

"Probably right," Ethan agreed. "OK, let's see—I think I have enough background info for now. What don't we talk about what you want to achieve?"

"Sounds good." Bud paused, collecting his thoughts. "What I *really* want is to bring this project in on time. I've had a lot of experiences to the contrary, and it would be nice to have this one finish on time."

"Yes, that would be nice," Ethan agreed, "and I know what you mean. Not sure if I can do anything about that, though."

"Yeah, I didn't really expect that you could. But that's ultimately what I want."

"I get that," Ethan said. "Is there another objective that I might be able to help you with?"

"Yes, there is, and it's the one we talked about earlier—I want to know if we're on schedule or not."

"A perfectly reasonable wish, I'd say, and it begs a question—why don't you know that already?"

Ethan waited for Bud to respond, and when that didn't happen, he continued. "I realize that may have sounded like an accusation, but I didn't mean it that way. What I'm saying is, there could be several perfectly good reasons why you don't know if you're on track. My question is, how would you describe your situation?"

This time Bud responded almost immediately. "Oh, I see. Well, it's like this–earlier this week I asked several of the people working on the project for their status. Some thought we were perhaps a week behind. Others thought we were on track. I wasn't happy with the fuzziness of the answers, so I started trying to see if I could measure the schedule status in some objective way. Then I got stuck, and eventually contacted you."

"OK, thanks for that," Ethan said. "Any idea why some folks think you're behind?"

"Yes, I believe so. It seems that the people who think we're behind have been working on tasks that took longer than expected."

"Is it as simple as that?" Ethan inquired.

"Yes, as far as I know, that's the sole reason for believing that we're behind."

"In that case, I have another question—what's your velocity?"

"I saw that one coming a mile away!" Bud nearly shouted. "That's why we're talking—I don't know."

"And do you think it would help to know that?"

"Yes, I do. But like I said before, we don't use 'points' for estimating, and I'm not sure how to express velocity using our estimation units."

"Well, then let's start from where you are. What are your units, again?" Ethan prompted.

"We estimated tasks in days."

"OK, then. One possibility that arises is that you could express your velocity in tasks per week. Does that sound like it might work?"

Bud mulled this over for a moment or two. "Sounds like it might, but it seems like that would work better if all the tasks were about the same size—they're not."

"How much is the variance," Ethan asked. "In other words, how big are your smallest and largest tasks?"

"We decided that no task would be smaller than a day. The largest task was estimated at five days."

"Ah, so projecting a schedule using tasks per week as your velocity wouldn't be very reliable."

"Guess not," Bud agreed. "I'd say that at any given moment we could be off by as much as a factor of five, depending on which tasks we had worked on that week."

"Yes, it would be like comparing apples to oranges, or perhaps apples to melons. Alright, then, let's try something else," Ethan suggested. "Since you use days instead of points, how about just expressing your velocity in *days per week*?"

"Days per week? You mean five?" Bud asked.

"No, I didn't, but I see why that's confusing. What I meant was, consider expressing your velocity in terms of how many days' worth of tasks you complete in a week."

"Oh, I see what you mean," Bud said slowly, not sure he liked the sound of it. "So, for example, if we get tasks A, B, C and D done in a week, and the estimates for those tasks totalled 4 days, our velocity would be 4 days per week."

"Yes, that's what I meant. Can't say I'm crazy about it, though," Ethan remarked.

"No, me neither," Bud said. "I'm imagining what it would be like to trying to convey that to my manager. He's likely to think that people are taking time off—you know, working only 4 days a week instead of 5."

"Yes, I know what you mean," Ethan said.

"And aside from that," Bud continued, "what about estimating in relative units, like in your workshop? Isn't that necessary to make this all work? All of our estimates are in absolute units."

"Well, I know you said you estimated in days," Ethan replied, "so you were thinking in absolute units when you made the estimates. But the relative units are in there, too."

"How do you mean?"

"Think of it this way—if you estimated one task at 1 day, and another task at 2 days, what you're saying is that the second task should take twice as long as the first one to complete. All you really need to do is stop calling them 'days' and you've got your relative units."

"Yeah, that makes sense," Bud said. "Hmm. Any reason why we can't just call them points, then?"

"None that I know of, at least not right now. And it seems to me that we may have enough information now for you to try to make an initial prediction of your completion date. Do you agree?"

Bud thought about it for a moment before responding. "No, I don't think so. I mean, I understand what we've covered so far, about how to express our velocity, and the relative units and such. That's all fine. The problem is, our situation is more complex than that. We've got five different groups working on this, and they've all made their own estimates. We work independently, but often in parallel. It's kind of a big jumble—I guess what I'm saying is, I'm having a hard time imagining how all of these things affect the overall schedule."

"Fair enough," Ethan replied. "And I think I may have some insights that you'll find useful. Unfortunately, I've got another call coming up in about five minutes. Do you have some free time on Monday to talk more about this?"

Bud started to check his calendar but, thinking better of it, responded, "Yes, absolutely!" This was important—if he had something else scheduled for Monday, he would move it.

"OK, then. I'll call you Monday morning about the same time, if that's OK."

"Perfect!" Bud replied. "I'm looking forward to it."

# 19

Bud busied himself with small tasks on Monday morning as he waited for Ethan's call. He had found it a little more difficult than usual to relax over the weekend—Friday's conversation had been encouraging, but decidedly incomplete.

He had spent a considerable amount of time, both waking and otherwise, going over the work situation in his head, trying to imagine some viewpoint that would bring it all into focus. He had been largely unsuccessful, and hoped that Ethan did indeed have some insights that would help them reliably figure out a completion date for the project.

As before, Bud's phone sounded at the appointed time. This time he answered it on the first ring.

"Hi, Ethan!"

"Hi, Bud. This still a good time to talk?"

"Couldn't be better," Bud replied. "What have you got for me?"

"Well, I thought I'd start by summarizing what I think this call is about, if that's OK."

"Yes, please do."

"The way I see it," Ethan began, "what we'd like to do is find a way for you to determine whether your project is on schedule. Do you agree?"

"Yes, that's it," Bud said, "If we can do that in this call, that would be great!"

"I think it's likely that we will—find a way, I mean. I don't believe we'll actually know if your project is on track by the end of the call, but we should be able to arrive at a way for you to find out."

"That would make me very happy."

"OK," Ethan said. "Let's get started. Now, as I recall, you said you've got five different groups working on your project."

"That's right."

"And although the groups work independently, some of the work takes place in parallel. For example—let me see—I'd guess that your user interface group does some design work, then feeds it to software development. Right so far?"

"Yes," Bud agreed, then added, "and then development eventually feeds it to testing."

"That's what I imagined," Ethan said. "The main thing I'm trying to establish here is that each group does only a piece of its own work before passing it along. The alternative approach would be that your user interface group would do all of its work first before turning anything over to development."

"No, we're definitely working in chunks."

"OK, that's good to know," Ethan remarked. "Now I remember you said that each of the groups did fairly detailed estimates prior to starting work."

"Yes, they did."

"I'm assuming that those estimates are still available somewhere?" It was more question than statement.

"Oh, yes, we've got all that. It took us the better part of a week to put together, so I made sure that we saved everything," Bud replied.

"Can you get at that easily?" Ethan asked. "What I'd be interested in knowing is whether one of the groups' estimated total time was substantially longer than that of any of the other groups."

Bud turned to his computer and began to retrieve the requested information. "I'm looking that up now. I don't remember the figures off the top of my head, but I do know that software development's total was the largest. Hang on—OK, here it is—yes, I remember now. Software development was estimated at 14 weeks. The next largest was testing, estimated at 7 weeks."

"That 14 week figure sounds familiar," Ethan said. "Didn't you tell me that the whole project was supposed to take about that long?"

"Yes, I think I mentioned that on Friday."

"That's interesting, "Ethan remarked. "Can you tell me why the two figures are the same?"

"Sure," Bud answered. "We figured that, in general, all of the groups would be working in parallel. Our reasoning was like this—if we *could* work completely in parallel, then the project time would be equal to the time taken by the group with the largest estimate."

"I see that," Ethan said. "I'm assuming that all of the work can't actually be done in parallel, but perhaps enough of it can so that the extra bits don't matter much."

"Yes, that was our assumption as well."

"Good," Ethan said. "Then I think we can move on. What I want to suggest is that, for the time being at least, we ignore the work of all except the software development group. Sound OK?"

"Suits me." Bud liked this simplification a lot.

"Now, as I recall, you said that you're about four weeks into the project. Is that right?"

"Yes, exactly right."

"Good. Now before we talk about the next step, I need to ask—in addition to the estimates you made, do you also have a record of the tasks completed so far?"

"Yes, we do," Bud replied. "Not only that, we know when each task was completed."

"That's perfect. We can use that. Now for that next step— you'll want to calculate your velocity."

"That I can do," Bud said. "Assuming each day is a 'point,' I can calculate our velocity in points per week based on what we've gotten done so far."

"That's right," Ethan agreed. "And you can probably tell me what the step after that is."

"Well, if I understand this correctly, the next step would be to calculate a completion date based on velocity and the number of points, or estimated days, remaining in the project. But it can't be that simple."

"Oh, I think it is," Ethan responded.

"But what about the work of all the other groups? Bud asked. "Are we just going to ignore that?"

"Perhaps," Ethan replied. "It depends."

"Depends on what?"

"On the answer we get from your completion date calculation."

"I think you lost me," Bud said.

"Look at it this way, "Ethan went on. "If you predict a completion date using only the software development estimates, and that date is past your deadline, then the project is late. Taking the other groups into account could only make it later, so it's still late."

"Ah, I see. And what if the predicted date is *before* the deadline?"

"Then we'll need to talk again," Ethan answered. "In the meantime, do you have any other questions before we hang up?"

"No, no I don't think so," Bud replied slowly. "I think I have everything I need."

"OK, good. Let me know if any questions come up."

"I will, and thanks!" Bud said. "I can't tell you how much I appreciate you spending your time on this."

Happy to help, Bud. Take care."

"You, too, Ethan. Bye."

Almost immediately, Bud sent an email to Ted Russell, inviting him for a chat.

# 20

Ted showed up in Bud's office about ten minutes later.

"Howdy, Bud."

"Hey, Ted. That was quick."

"Yeah, well, I saw your email just as I was leaving for lunch. Thought I'd drop by on my way out. What's up?"

"I was hoping you and I could pair up to do some calculations around the project schedule," Bud replied.

"Is this about the schedule slippage?" Ted asked, somewhat warily.

"Yes, in a way, but there's more to it than that. I want to generate some information about the completion date, and to do that I need to do some calculations using some of the task data we've collected. Want to help with that?"

"Yes, I do!" Ted's response was enthusiastic. "Did you want to start right away, or can I grab some lunch first?"

"No, go ahead and get lunch—we can start when you get back."

"OK, thanks," Ted said. "I'll make it a quick one."

True to his word, Ted arrived back in Bud's office about twenty minutes later, laptop in hand.

"Welcome back," Bud said. "Ready to get started?"

"Ready, chief." Ted was in a good mood.

"OK, then. Let me tell you what I'd like to do," Bud began. "I'd like to be able to figure out if we're behind schedule on the FutureCash project and, if so, by how much."

"Sounds straightforward enough," Ted offered. "Any idea how you want to go about that?"

"Yes, I believe so. I want to compare how much we thought we'd have done by now to how much we've *actually* done."

"So you'll need to see our estimates," Ted volunteered.

"Yes," Bud agreed, "the estimates, plus the data we've collected about when each task was completed."

"No problem on either count. Just give me a couple of minutes to find that stuff." Ted busied himself at his laptop, eventually locating the requested information.

"OK, I'm looking at the estimates," he announced. "What's next?"

"How about a quick review of the task breakdown we did?" Bud asked.

"Alright, let's see," Ted responded. "Looks like we ended up with a total estimate of 71 days."

"And how many tasks did we have altogether?"

"Says here, 55."

"Yes, that sounds right," Bud said. "And one other thing— what were our smallest and largest tasks?"

Ted took a while scanning the data before responding. "The smallest I see is 1 day. The largest is 5."

"Good. That matches my recollection." Bud pondered the next step before continuing. "I think what I'd like to do next is create a spreadsheet to summarize the work we've done so far. For that we'll need the task completion data."

"Got it right here," Ted stated.

"OK, good. How about if I drive for a minute or two?"

Ted shoved the laptop over so that Bud could use it.

Bud talked to himself as he filled in the new spreadsheet. "I'll want to know which week each task was completed in. Then there's our original estimate for how many points we expected to get done each week..."

"Points?" Ted interjected. "What are points?"

Bud looked up suddenly. "Oh, yeah, sorry—I forgot you weren't involved in that conversation. There's a reason, that I can explain later, for expressing our estimates in something other than days. I'm going to call them 'points,' but they're exactly the same as our estimates in days."

"You're the boss," Ted said. "But in either case, aren't all of the weekly estimates the same?"

"How do you mean?"

"Well, we assumed that we could get 5 days worth of work done every week..."

"Oh, right," Bud said. "So that's 5 points each week, then." He added some more figures to the spreadsheet. "And I'm going to total that while I'm at it. Yes, that's right—5 points per week times 4 week equals 20 estimated points.

"Now we'll want to know how many points we actually got done each week."

"That information is in the other spreadsheet," Ted said, pointing to the computer screen.

"Ah, thanks." Bud typed in a few more numbers. "Might as well total that now, too. Looks like we actually got 15 points completed in the first 4 weeks.

"Now let me just do some calculations—I'll want to calculate how much slippage there was each week, and get a total." After a little more data entry, he announced, "Looks like you were right, Ted, when you said we were about a week behind."

Ted looked where Bud was pointing. The total slippage after 4 weeks of work was 5 days.

| Week | Estimated Points | Actual Points | Slippage |
|---|---|---|---|
| 1 | 5 | 4 | 1 |
| 2 | 5 | 4 | 1 |
| 3 | 5 | 3 | 2 |
| 4 | 5 | 4 | 1 |
| Total: | 20 | 15 | 5 |

"Pretty good for just guessing," Ted beamed. "Is that what you wanted to know?"

"That's the first part," Bud replied. "Now I want to do a projection based on our velocity."

"Uh, 'velocity?' You'll have to clue me in."

"Velocity is the rate at which we get work done. In this case we can express it in units of points per week."

"OK." Ted's expression changed from one of puzzlement to one of understanding. "Oh, so this is why we're using 'points,'" he declared. *Days per week* would be confusing."

"Exactly so," Bud confirmed. He busied himself with the spreadsheet once again. "In this case, that's just an average of the total points completed, which in this case is 15 divided by 4, or 3.75 points per week."

"Looks right," Ted agreed. "I think I see where you're going with this."

"Now," Bud continued, nodding his head, "all we need to do is calculate how many weeks it would take at that rate to get our original 71 points done. That's just a simple division." He fiddled with the spreadsheet some more.

| Total Points | Points per Week | Total Weeks |
|:---:|:---:|:---:|
| 71 | 3.75 | **18.9** |

Both men stared at the spreadsheet for quite some time before Ted broke the silence. "Can that be right?"

Bud pondered the result for a while longer, reworking the calculation in his head before responding. "Yes, the figures are correct."

"But our original estimate was 14 weeks!" Ted exclaimed. "This says almost 19 weeks—that means we're 5 weeks behind!"

"Yes, yes it does," Bud agreed.

"But we've only slipped by 5 *days*."

"Yes, that's true," Bud responded. "And ordinarily what I'd do is just add that 5 days to the end of the current schedule and say we're a week behind."

"Sounds good—let's do that," Ted suggested, only half joking.

"Don't think we can," Bud said. "Not with this information staring us in the face."

"Man, this isn't good," Ted declared. Still hopeful, he added, "Well, maybe we can still catch up."

"Maybe." Bud considered the problem. "We may run up against a speed limit problem, though."

Ted waited in silence for Bud to explain.

"What I mean is," Bud continued, "there's an upper limit to the amount of work we can get done in a week. Looking over the figures, I see that the most points we ever completed in a given week was 4. Do we have any reason to believe that we can do better than that?"

"I'm not sure," Ted replied. "Our velocity could increase now that we're past that snag we encountered with the graphics library. That was in week three, by the way."

"OK, let's consider that. Let's see what kind of velocity we would need in order to get back on the original schedule." Bud returned to the spreadsheet and entered some more data, talking as he went.

"Our original schedule was 14 weeks. We've worked for 4 weeks already, so that leaves 10 weeks remaining. We started out with 71 points, and we've completed 15 points so far, so that means we need to complete 56 more points of work in that time. That comes to 5.6 points per week."

| Weeks Remaining | Points to Complete | Points per Week |
|:---:|:---:|:---:|
| 10 | 56 | **5.6** |

"It doesn't seem so bad when you look at it that way," Ted suggested.

"No, it's a little bit easier to swallow," Bud admitted. "Question is, can we do it?"

Ted considered the question. "You know, Bud, I have no idea."

"I don't either," Bud said slowly, eventually adding, "but I know a way to find out."

"Oh, good." Ted seemed relieved. "How?"

"We have to 'eat some fruit.'"

"Say again?"

"Sorry," Bud went on. "What I mean is, the best way I know to find the upper limit of our velocity is simply to keep working. If the rate goes up, we'll know there's a possibility that we can catch up, at least some."

"I see what you mean," Ted said. "OK, then. Is there anything else I can do?"

"No, just keep at it I think. As for me, I'd better go have a talk with Bob Harvey."

# 21

A voice from the hallway called out, "Talk with Bob Harvey about what?" It was Bob Harvey.

Bud and Ted looked up just as Bob appeared in the doorway.

"Hi, Bob," Bud said. "I was just going to look for you."

"So I heard," Bob replied, smiling. "I was just on my way to my office—want to walk with me?"

"Sure." Turning to Ted, Bud said, "Just business as usual, then. Let's continue to track progress as we have been, and we can talk again later."

"Sounds good," Ted responded. "See you later. See you, Bob."

"OK, Ted."

Bud followed Bob to his office. Bob walked at a brisk pace, and Bud found himself trailing behind by about half a step for most of the short journey.

"Have a seat, Bud," Bob offered as he took up residence behind his desk. "What's on your mind?"

"Well," Bud began as he sat, "I wanted to speak with you about the status of the FutureCash project."

"I imagined as much. How's that going?"

"Fairly well, I'd say. We're making progress. What I want to talk with you about is the schedule. I've been doing some projections—Ted and I were just finishing up when you dropped by—and right now it looks like we're not going to make our scheduled completion date."

"Yes, I've heard rumblings about some minor slippages. Do you have any reason to believe that they're more than minor?"

"Well, yes and no," Bud replied. "Our figures show that we've slipped five days in the first four weeks of the project."

"Doesn't sound so bad."

"No, you're right, it doesn't," Bud agreed. "But our projection of the completion date says that we're actually about five weeks behind."

Bob looked lost in thought for a moment. "Are you telling me that, four weeks into the project, we're already five weeks behind?"

"Well, I suppose you could put it that way. Sounds impossible, though, doesn't it? No, I think the way I'd express it is, if we continue to get work done at the present rate, then we'll finish about five weeks after the desired completion date."

"Ah, well that makes a little more sense, anyway," Bob said. "Mind telling me how you arrived at your figures?"

"No, not at all," Bud replied, "and I can show you the spreadsheets if that would help. Essentially what we did was compare two velocities. One is the rate at which we are actually getting work done. The other is the rate we would need to achieve in order to get the work done on time."

"I see. And I take it that the measured velocity figure is somewhat less than the ideal one?" Bob made quotes with his fingers when he said the word *velocity*.

"Exactly," Bud replied.

"Remind me—how long did we anticipate the project taking?"

"Our initial estimate was fourteen weeks."

"And so now we're looking at nineteen weeks?"

"Roughly, yes."

"Can we pick up the pace?" Bob inquired. "How much overtime are people working at this point?"

"Not much, I think. Marj put in some extra time a week or two ago but, as far as I know, people are mostly putting in standard work weeks."

"Well, that's good," Bob said. "Looks like we have that option if we need it."

Bud hesitated just a bit before proceeding to the next topic. "The thing is," he began, "I think we should talk about how we might proceed in the event that we can't 'pick up the pace.'"

Bob raised his eyebrows, signalling Bud to continue.

"What I mean is," Bud went on, "it seems like it would be wise to consider which features in FutureCash we're willing to drop in order to finish on time."

Bob frowned slightly. "Well, I'm not sure about that, but I know how marketing will feel about it. They've been talking up the benefits of FutureCash with a bunch of our existing clients. I'm pretty sure they're not going to be happy delivering a subset of those benefits."

"So you're OK with the project finishing behind schedule?"

"Well, I wouldn't say that, exactly. What I'd like to see is for all of the features of FutureCash to be delivered on time."

"Yes, and so would I," Bud agreed. "But what if that's not possible—which trade-off would you prefer to make?"

Bob remained silent for an almost uncomfortably long time before answering. "Bud, you haven't been in the management end of things for very long."

"About three years," Bud confirmed.

"And you've been at FiscalWare for how long?"

"Just over six months."

"Uh-huh. Well, I'm not sure how many times you've personally encountered this situation we're talking about, but let me assure you that this happens all the time. Projects are always behind schedule. Marketing always promises things to customers before they're built. And development always wants to know which features can be cut."

"Yes," Bud responded, "I'm familiar. This happened all the time at my last company, too."

"You see? This is normal. It's been going on for as long as I can remember, anyway. Marketing comes in with a whole list of features that they believe the customers want, and they assure the customers that those features are what they'll get. Development looks at the list of features and estimates how long it will take to deliver them—the estimates are usually optimistic. Marketing repeats the optimistic delivery date to the customers, then development begins and almost immediately falls behind. Eventually someone goes to management and asks if features can be cut. It's a common pattern."

Bud was mesmerized. He had been vaguely aware of the various aspects of what Bob had described, but had never before heard it encapsulated as Bob had just done.

"I know what you mean," Bud eventually replied. "I've seen this happen before, too. It's just that I tend to believe we should be able to do better than that."

Bob's smile made Bud think that he was going to get a pat on the head before being told to run along.

"That would be nice," Bob said. "But let me give you some more information before we go there."

"OK."

"First, about the schedule—I think that a five week delay in completion is not so bad, but I'd prefer to keep it under that if possible. The market window we talked about before the project started is wide enough to accommodate that much of a delay, but probably not more.

"Second, about cutting features—that could turn into a real fight with marketing. As I said, they've already talked up the benefits of FutureCash to most of our customers. A stripped-down version would almost certainly reduce the number of sales we would make.

"What I would do, if I were you, is try to get the project back on schedule. Get people to work some overtime. Find ways to motivate them to meet their commitments. That kind of thing."

"OK, I hear what you're saying," Bud responded. "No feature cuts, and limited schedule delay."

"Right!" Bob said enthusiastically. "By the way, thanks for bringing this to my attention. Now let's see if we can get this project back on track."

# 22

Bud wandered back toward his office, trying to make some sense of the exchange that had just occurred. He was still puzzling over it when Ted Russell appeared beside him.

"Hey, Bud. How'd it go?"

"Hey, Ted. I'm not sure."

"That bad, huh?"

"No, no I wouldn't say bad, necessarily—I'm just not sure what I'm supposed to do now."

"What did Bob say?"

The two men eventually arrived at Bud's office, where they sat and continued the conversation.

"Basically he said that I should try to find ways to motivate you guys to work some overtime," Bud replied.

"More overtime?"

"Well, he didn't say 'more.' Are you working overtime now?"

"Yes, some. Offhand I'd say that every developer on the project is putting in an extra hour or two every day on it," Ted answered. "And on top of that," he went on, "it's not as if FutureCash is the only thing we have to do—we've got two other active projects with deadlines of their own."

"Yeah, I know that." Bud was sympathetic.

"So what did Bob say about us being behind schedule?" Ted asked.

"Oh, that kind of surprised me—he said that the market window could accommodate the five-week delay we're currently predicting, but not more than that."

"Really? That surprises me, too" Ted volunteered. "Well, aren't we OK, then?"

"Again, I'm not sure. It would be nice to get the project a little more on track than it is right now—at least we'd have some breathing room."

"Yeah, I know what you mean," Ted agreed. After a while he added, "So what are you going to do?"

Bud had made up his mind. "I'm going to ask for help," he declared.

Ted waited patiently for the explanation he knew would be forthcoming.

"I'm going to give Ethan a call."

"The guy from the conference?"

"That's the one," Bud confirmed. "Want to hang around while I see if he's available?"

"Yes, I certainly do."

It took Bud a minute to locate Ethan's phone number. Ethan picked up on the third ring.

"Hi, Bud. What can I do for you?"

"Hi, Ethan. Sorry to just call out of the blue like this. Do you have a few minutes?"

"I have a meeting in about half an hour, and I have a little prep to do for that. I can spare ten or fifteen minutes."

"OK, thanks—I'll get right to it, then. By the way, I've got you on speaker—Ted Russell is here with me."

"Hello, Ted."

"Hey, Ethan. Pleased to meet you."

"Same here."

Bud went on. "Now, I don't know if you remember our last conversation..."

"As I recall," Ethan jumped in, "You were going to calculate a velocity for the development work you've done so far."

Bud wondered, not for the first time, how Ethan was able to retain that kind of information and recall it, seemingly at will. "Yes, that's right," he replied. "Our velocity so far averages 3.75 points per week and, using that information, we projected that our project will take a total of nineteen weeks to complete, instead of the fourteen weeks we predicted earlier."

"I understand," Ethan acknowledged. "Did you find that information helpful?"

"Well, yes—it was a good reality check. I've just had a conversation with my boss, and he's urging me to try to get the project back on track."

"Yes, that's understandable," Ethan responded. "What can I do for you?"

"Well," Bud ventured, "can you help me get the project back on track?"

Ethan chuckled. "That would be nice, wouldn't it? I'm not sure about that. Mind if I ask you a couple of questions?"

"Ask away."

"OK. I seem to remember that you were using *days* for *points*. Is that right?"

"Yes, that's right," Bud replied.

"Alright, then. I'd be curious to know if your projection comes out about the same if you use points like we did in the exercise at the conference. Remember the Fibonacci numbers?"

"Yes, I remember," Bud said. "But our estimates weren't done that way."

"I know. What I'm suggesting is that you estimate again, this time the way we did in the exercise."

A long pause ensued while Bud attempted to understand the full implications of Ethan's suggestion.

"I'm not sure we can afford that," Bud said finally. "It took us the better part of a week to come up with estimates before. I'm a little reluctant to spend that kind of time now, especially since we're behind schedule already."

"I hear you," Ethan said. " I wouldn't want to invest a week doing this either. But I don't think you'll have to."

"I'm all ears."

"Before I go on, "Ethan said, "remind me—how many development tasks did you make estimates for?"

Bud knew that figure by heart. "There are fifty-five development tasks in total."

"OK, good. Now what would you say if I told you that you can estimate all of those inside the space of half a day?"

"I'd say 'tell me more.'"

"Then I will. I've collected quite a bit of data on this, informally. In general, the people I've worked with have been able to make estimates at the rate of from one to three minutes per task."

"Are you talking about estimating eating fruit?" Bud asked, a little skeptically.

"It turns out that it doesn't make much of a difference," Ethan replied. "The results are pretty much the same whether people are estimating fruit consumption or serious, technical tasks."

"Well, I'm certainly willing to try it, if I can get Ted to go along with it. Ted?"

"I'm up for it," Ted replied. "What do I have to do?"

"Bud can instruct you on how the estimation technique works," Ethan said. "Bud, I'm going to send you a file by email that contains all the cards for the estimation exercise you did at the conference. You can print those out yourself.

"I suggest that you teach Ted, and anyone else who's going to be estimating, the technique using the fruit cards before you do it for real with your actual development tasks."

"'Anyone else?'" Ted jumped in. "Who else would there be?"

"Ah, yes, we haven't talked about this yet, have we?" Ethan responded. "Let me ask you, then—who was doing your estimating before?"

"You mean in the software development group?" Ted asked.

"Yes, just in your group."

"Well, Bud and me."

"OK," Ethan continued. "Are Bud and you the only ones doing the development work?"

"No, not at all," Ted replied. "In fact, Bud doesn't really do any of the development work. He's managing the project."

Ethan pressed on. "So there are other people doing development work?"

"Yes. We've got three other developers on this project— Ursula, Vince and William."

"In that case, I'd suggest that Bud teach you and the other three the estimation technique," Ethan said. "Things seem to work out better when the people doing the work are also the ones who estimate the work."

"OK, that makes sense," Ted agreed. "I'll see if I can get all of us together. Tomorrow morning work for you, Bud? Oh, and how long do you think it'll take?"

"Yes, it does, and about 90 minutes," Bud answered. "In the meantime, I'll arrange to have our actual work tasks printed on cards, too, just to get ready."

"Good idea," Ethan agreed. "Anything else before we hang up?"

"Not that I can think of," Bud replied. "Thanks again for taking the time to talk about this. It's been a big help."

"Glad to do it. And give me a call after you've got your new estimates. I've got something else you may find useful."

"I definitely will. Take care."

Bud hung up the phone and smiled at Ted. "Well, we have a direction. I'll see about getting those task cards printed up."

"And I'll round up the other developers for tomorrow," Ted said. "This should be interesting."

# 23

A couple of days later, Bud and Ted again found themselves in Bud's office, tabulating information they'd recently gathered.

The two estimation sessions, one to teach the developers the technique in the abstract, and the other to estimate their actual work tasks, had gone smoothly.

"It looks like Ethan was right," Bud remarked. "Hard to believe that we could estimate all of those tasks in just three hours when it took almost a week the first time around."

"I know what you mean," Ted agreed. "And it turned out to be pretty entertaining besides. I was concerned for a while that we'd gotten into an infinite loop when Ursula and William kept moving the pineapple card back and forth between the same two columns. How may rounds of that were there?"

"I stopped counting at five," Bud replied. "And I thought it was interesting to see how everyone seemed to engage so earnestly in the learning exercise. No one 'phoned it in,' even though they were only working with fruit."

"Yeah, I noticed that, too. Funny, huh?"

"So where are we?" Bud asked, changing gears. "Why don't we review the new totals first?"

"Sure, they're right here." Ted pointed to a spreadsheet. "It looks like, based on the new estimates, the number of points for our 55 tasks totals 933. That seems like a lot."

"Yes, it does," Bud agreed. "What were our minimum and maximum estimates?"

"Hang on—OK, it looks like our smallest estimate was 3, and the largest was 34."

"Now that's curious," Bud mused. "When we estimated these same tasks in days, our minimum was 1, and our maximum was

5. That's a ratio of 5 to 1. Now it looks like our ratio of largest to smallest is about 10 to 1. I wonder what that's about."

Ted scratched his head a bit before responding. "I think I may know. Remember, when we estimated these tasks in days, we decided that the minimum task size would be one day. Now, I can't speak for you, but when I was doing the original estimates, there were some tasks that I thought of as being half-day efforts—but we restricted ourselves to that one-day minimum, so I just assigned a whole day to each of those half-day tasks."

"Yes, I guess that could explain it," Bud said. "Now that I think of it, I did some of that 'rounding' myself."

"Fair enough. So what's next?"

"Let's see if we can calculate our velocity for the first four weeks of work, like we did before." Bud suggested.

"Alright, let's see," Ted said. "In the first four weeks, we completed 220 points, giving us an average velocity of 55 points per week.

| Week | Points |
|------|--------|
| 1 | 55 |
| 2 | 63 |
| 3 | 44 |
| 4 | 58 |
| Total: | 220 |
| Average Velocity: | 55 |

"OK, then," Bud went on, "the next thing we need to do is project a completion date based on that."

"We did that same thing with the previous figures," Ted said. "Just let me plug the new numbers in...OK, it looks like, with a total of 933 points at a velocity of 55 points per week, the total completion time is 16.9 weeks."

| Total Points | Points per Week | Total Weeks |
|:---:|:---:|:---:|
| 933 | 55 | **16.9** |

"I believe our old estimates put that at 19 weeks," Bud said.

"Yes, just under," Ted confirmed. "Well, what do you know?" Ted continued. "Looks like we've saved a couple of weeks, just by re-estimating. Is that possible?"

"Oh, sure," Bud joked. "Perhaps if we just keep re-estimating we can get the project done in no time at all."

The two men grew quiet as they considered the implications of the information before them.

It was Bud who spoke first. "No, I don't think there's any mystery here. See if this makes sense. Imagine that when we originally estimated the first four weeks of tasks, we *underestimated* them, relative to the tasks remaining in the project. If that were the case, it follows that the velocity figure for the first four weeks would be smaller, therefore our projection was for a longer completion time."

"I follow," Ted said. "And likewise, if we have *overestimated* the first four weeks of tasks this time—meaning we've assigned them higher point values relative to the remaining tasks—then our velocity figure would be higher, making it appear as if we've gotten a proportionately greater amount of the project done already."

"Exactly, "Bud concurred.

"So, which is right, then?" Ted asked.

"Good question. Honestly, I don't think we can know that yet—but I suppose that if we continue to track velocity from week to week, we'll know soon enough. Seems to me that the closer our estimates are to being correct, relative to each other of course, the more stable our velocity figure will remain from week to week."

"That *sounds* right," Ted said slowly. "I guess I'll need to think about it a little more before I'm completely convinced."

"Yeah, me too," Bud admitted. "Anyway, I think there's one more piece of information that we want to look at right now."

"Way ahead of you, Bud. You're talking about what velocity we would need to get the project back on the original schedule?"

"Indeed," Bud replied. "Got those figures handy?"

Ted fiddled with the spreadsheet. "Yes—just like before, we have 10 weeks remaining out of the original 14-week schedule. We've completed 220 out of 933 points in the first four weeks, so that leaves 713 points. That means we'd have to average 71.3 points per week for the rest of the project in order to get completely back on track."

| Weeks Remaining | Points to Complete | Points per Week |
|---|---|---|
| 10 | 713 | **71.3** |

"I agree with the calculations," Bud said eventually. "Question is, can we reasonably expect to increase our velocity from 55 to 71?"

"I have no opinion on that whatsoever," Ted replied. "Looks like we're just going to have to 'eat some more fruit.'"

"My thoughts exactly," Bud agreed. "So, next steps—I'd say it's time to give Ethan another call."

"Oh, right. He asked us to let him know when we had the new figures. And I've been curious about that 'something useful' since he mentioned it last time."

"I'm with you on that," Bud concurred. "Let's see if he's in."

# 24

Bud dialed Ethan Green's number, and was immediately taken to voicemail. Ethan called back before Bud was able to leave an entire message.

"Hi, Ethan," Bud said. "I was just talking to your voicemail. How are you?"

"Fine, Bud, thanks. Sorry for not picking up—I was just finishing up another call."

"No problem, really," Bud assured him. "By the way, I've got Ted here with me again, and you're on speaker."

"That's fine. Hi, Ted."

"Hey, Ethan."

"What can I do for you both?" Ethan asked. "Do you have the new projections ready?"

"Yes, we just finished compiling them," Bud replied. "Got a few minutes?"

"I do," Ethan replied. "Nothing pressing for the rest of the day, as it turns out, so I'm all yours."

"Good. OK, let's see. We re-estimated using relative numbers, like in your exercise, and we got a new total—933 points for the entire set of 55 tasks."

"Alright."

"Then we calculated our velocity based on the work we've done so far—it's averaging 55 points per week."

"Good."

"So," Bud continued, "we're projecting a total project duration of about 17 weeks. Still greater than the 14 weeks we wanted, but less than the 19 weeks we projected when we estimated last time."

"I understand," Ethan said. "What do you plan to do next, if I may ask?"

"Our only plan for now is to 'eat some more fruit.'"

Ethan chuckled. "Yes, that's what I'd be doing. Any ideas about how you'll keep track of your progress as you go?"

"Well," Bud answered slowly, "we've been keeping all of this information in a spreadsheet, so I guess we'll continue to do that."

"That sounds fine," Ethan agreed. "You may think of all kinds of calculations you could perform on the data, and having it in a spreadsheet will certainly make that easy. I've got a suggestion for something you can do on top of that to help you visualize your schedule."

"That would be nice," Ted chimed in. "Suggest away!"

"Have you worked with burndown charts before?"

Bud and Ted looked at each other, each man's curious expression mirroring the other's. Bud was the first to respond. "We have, but how did you know? That information is supposed to be proprietary."

"Not sure what you mean, Bud. Are you saying that you have burndown charts in your product?"

"Yes, we do. But I don't remember mentioning that."

"No, I don't think you did."

"Anyway, no harm in telling you," Bud went on. "In essence we use them to tell the user when he's going to run out of money. It's a lot easier to see that in chart form than it is in a list of numbers."

"I agree," Ethan said. "You ought to understand this immediately, then. In this case we're going to use a burndown chart to tell you when you're going to 'run out of points.'"

"Ah, I know where you're going with this!" Ted exclaimed.

Bud nodded, but let Ted go on.

"I'm guessing that we're going to create a chart with 'points' on the Y axis and 'weeks' on the X axis." He picked up a piece of paper and began sketching as he spoke.

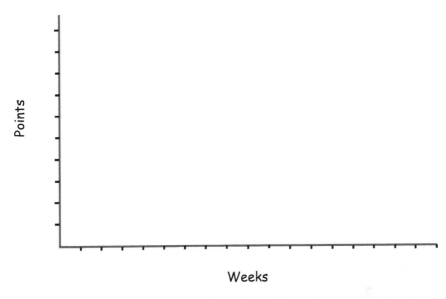

Weeks

"Yes, that's right," Bud said. "Then all we have to do is chart our weekly progress, and we'll be able to see our projected completion time at a glance."

"Way ahead of you," Ted said. "Let's see—we started with 933 points, and in the first week we completed 55 so, subtracting one from the other, we get 878. Another 63 points completed in the second week gives us 815. Only 44 in the third gives us 771, and 58 in the fourth week gives us 713."

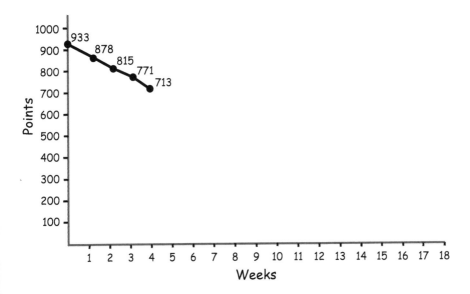

Weeks

124

"How does it look?" Ethan asked.

"Oh, sorry, Ethan," Bud replied. "I got so involved in charting our figures that I forgot you were there. It looks good—the velocity seems pretty steady at this scale."

"Do you have a line connecting your data points?"

"Yes, we do."

"OK, then. Now how about projecting that line all the way to the X axis?"

Ted hunted around for something to use as a straightedge, finally selecting a legal pad that Bud kept on his desk. "OK, I've got a dashed line that continues where our data left off. It hits the X axis at about 17 weeks."

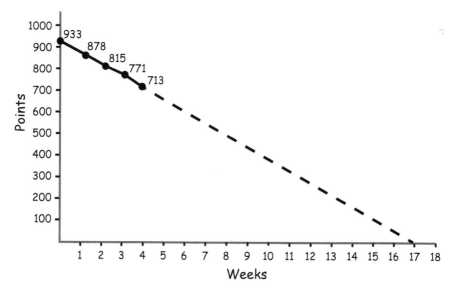

"Very good," Ethan said. "What are you drawing on, by the way?"

"Just a piece of printer paper," Ted answered. "But I can arrange to generate this same chart in our spreadsheet and it'll look a lot cleaner."

"Well, then, I have another suggestion. Have you got some flip-chart paper around? You know—the stuff you usually find on an easel in the corner of a conference room?"

"Tons of it." Bud replied. "We use flip-charts in meetings all the time. I think we may even have some with grid lines."

"That would be perfect," Ethan said. "My suggestion is that you reproduce the chart you just made, but larger, using the flip-chart paper, and post it in a prominent location so that anyone who's interested can see it as they walk by."

"Yeah, I can do that." Ted volunteered. "We can put it up in the space where the developers work. There's a lot of foot traffic through there."

"Sounds just right, "Ethan remarked.

"Mind if I ask the about the reason for posting the chart?" Bud inquired.

"No, not at all," Ethan replied. "I think you'll find your own reasons after the chart is up for a while, but for now let's just say that making the schedule information visible should have some positive effects. This kind of transparency tends to make people, especially those in management, less nervous about project status, since they can see it any time they like."

"OK, I follow that. We'll give it a try."

"I have a question," Ted said. "How often should we update the chart?"

"I think that weekly should be often enough for now," Ethan answered. "Technically you could update it after each task is completed. I'd experiment if I were you and find out what works best."

"OK, thanks," Ted said. "Anything else we should know?"

"I can't think of anything at the moment," Ethan replied. "Have fun with the charting, and let me know if any questions come up."

"Will do," Bud said. "And thanks again, Ethan, for all your help. I'll let you know how things go."

"Please do. I'm looking forward to our next talk. So long."

"Bye."

Bud and Ted looked at each other, smiling.

"I feel like we've made some real progress here," Bud said eventually. "I certainly like the idea of being able to see how the project is going at a glance."

"I agree," Ted said. "This picture is worth at least a thousand words—to me, anyway. I'm curious, though—do you think anyone aside from us will get this?"

"No idea," Bud replied, "but I know a way to find out."

"I'm with you," Ted agreed. "I'll go dig up some flip-chart paper."

# 25

The FutureCash project was just over ten weeks along, and Bud and Ted found themselves in a weekly meeting that had become a regular part of the way they worked together.

Ted was in the middle of a summation about progress made and progress anticipated. "...so it looks like we've actually gained some ground over the last six weeks. Back then, it looked like we would finish in a total of seventeen weeks. Now that's down to about fifteen and a half."

"Yes, I'm aware," Bud said. "I've been following the burndown chart. I must say, though, that this is not what I expected. Quite the opposite in fact—I expected that we would get farther and farther behind with time."

"I know what you mean," Ted responded. "This isn't the usual pattern in my experience, either. I'm not complaining, though—I've even found myself thinking that we might actually be able to get back to the original project schedule."

"I like your optimism," Bud said. "For my part, I'd be happy to stay right where we are, schedule-wise. I keep waiting for some roadblock that will negate all the progress we've made so far."

"Yeah, I hear you. But we can only do what we can do."

"Always the philosopher," Bud remarked with a slight smile. "Anyway, let's talk about this. Got any ideas about why we seem to be gaining ground?"

"Well, nothing solid, but I do have some theories. Want to hear them?"

"Absolutely."

"OK, here goes. The first thing that occurs to me is that our estimates may have been heavy on the front end and light on the back end, if you follow me."

"I think so," Bud said. "It's much like the issue we talked about when we decided to re-estimate all the tasks using Fibonacci numbers. Back then we considered the idea that our original estimates might be heavy, and that the new ones might be light."

"Yes, same idea," Ted confirmed. "Only this time, all the estimates use the same numbers. The difference, if there is one, would come from estimating heavy for tasks that are earlier in the schedule and light for those occurring later in the schedule."

"How likely do you think that is?" Bud inquired.

"Now that I hear it out loud, not very. Seems to me that it would take a pretty large coincidence to make it so that our 'weighted' estimates just happened to give us a steady gain over time like we're seeing."

"Yeah, I tend to agree with you," Bud said. "Any more theories?"

"Yes. This next one is a bit more complex. It has to do with something I've observed while working with the other developers. I've seen a change in the way they all work. No, I mean the way *we* all work—I include myself in this—since we changed to this new way of estimating."

"Now I'm intrigued," Bud interjected.

"It's a little hard to describe," Ted went on, "but I'd say there's a difference in our attitudes about finishing tasks. We all seem a lot more eager now to finish each task as soon as possible and move on to the next one."

"Is it like a contest in some way?" Bud asked.

"No, I wouldn't say so. It doesn't feel like a competition—it's more like getting a reward for completion."

Bud waited in silence as Ted gathered his thoughts. This was getting interesting.

Eventually, Ted continued. "When each task was associated with a number of days of effort, we'd work on it and eventually it would be done—those days would be behind us. Now, however, when we complete a task we get to claim a certain number of points completed, and we can actually see the progress we've made right then and there."

"On the burndown chart." Bud offered.

"Yes, exactly. Oh, and by the way, have you seen the new chart—the one down the hall from the project burndown chart?"

"Can't say I've noticed it."

"Well, you should have a look when you get a chance. Ursula, Vince and William weren't satisfied with updating the burndown chart only once a week, so they posted a new one and are using it to track their day-to-day progress."

"Why did they need a new chart for that?"

"The old chart is a burndown of the entire project. The new one shows just a week of activity," Ted replied.

"And they're updating it daily?" Bud asked.

"Actually, they're updating it very time they finish a task. You should drop by from time to time and give it a look."

"I definitely will," Bud responded. "So you think work is actually getting done faster because of this?"

"Well, like I said, it's a theory. Work does seem to be getting done faster, in any case. Our velocity figure has grown steadily over the past six weeks."

"Yes, so it seems," Bud said cautiously. "Is that it?"

"No, I've got one more—a related theory, but along somewhat the same line."

"Do tell."

"Happy to, but first let me ask you something—do you remember when you were working as a developer?"

"Certainly. It wasn't that long ago."

"And do you also remember," Ted continued, "what it was like to be assigned tasks and told how long you had to complete them?"

"Indeed I do," Bud replied. "Between you and me, that was probably one of the main reasons I got into management. As a developer I had little say in creating the work schedules. There was always somebody above me who told me how long I *should* be spending on each bit of work."

"And do you remember ever completing a task ahead of time?"

Bud thought for a while before answering. "Well, there may have been a few times when that happened, but mostly I remember using all of the time allotted for each task—and then some. Some tasks got completed on time, but it was also very common for tasks to take longer than the schedule allowed."

"That's been my experience, too," Ted concurred, "until recently. Now things are different."

"How so?"

"Glad you asked," Ted kidded. "Think about this—when I start to work on a task now, how much time do I have in which to complete it?"

Bud opened his mouth, then closed it again. It was a few moments before the idea that Ted was trying to convey began to sink in. "Oh, I see what you mean. If you had asked me that back when we were estimating in absolute time, I would have answered something like 'three days.' Now that we're estimating in relative time, the only possible answer would be something like 'thirteen points,' which doesn't make sense—it certainly doesn't answer the question."

"Exactly," Ted said. "These days there isn't any chunk of time allotted for completing a task, so instead of working on a task until all the time is used up, we simply work on a task until it's done, then move on."

"'Work expands so as to fill the time available for its completion,'" Bud quoted. "Parkinson's law."

"Right," Ted confirmed. "In our case the time available for completion is unknown. I think that's a benefit."

"It's a beautiful theory," Bud declared.

Ted beamed. "I have my moments."

"Anything else before we adjourn, then?" Bud asked.

"Not that I can think of. And you really should drop by to see the new burndown chart."

"Good idea. Think I'll do that now."

# 26

Fourteen weeks had been a significant milestone for the FutureCash project from the beginning and, even though most of the people working on the project had given up any expectations of it finishing by that time, when it eventually did arrive it meant to many that the project was now officially late.

Bob Harvey was one of the many, and he chose that day to invite Bud to his office to talk it over.

"Good to see you, Bud. Come on in."

"Hi Bob. Thanks." Bud took a seat near Bob's desk and waited for him to start.

"I imagine you're wondering why I called you here," Bob began.

"I expect it's about the FutureCash schedule," Bud ventured.

"Yes, that's it. Today is the official end-of-project, as I'm sure you know."

"Of course. And we're not done yet."

"Nor did I expect us to be—and that's what I want to talk to you about."

Bud waited patiently while Bob appeared to collect his thoughts.

"First," Bob went on, "I want to say that I'm impressed by what you've done—very impressed."

"Thanks." Bud waited for Bob to elaborate.

"I think I should tell you that when you and I talked about this more than three months ago, I didn't have any illusions about the reliability of your estimate."

"You mean the 'ballpark' estimate—the one you weren't going to hold me to?" Bud asked.

"Yes, that's the one. And I meant it when I said I wasn't going to hold you to it."

"As I recall, it was only a week later that my ballpark estimate appeared on the internal website."

"Yes, that's how I remember it as well," Bob confirmed. Seeing the look of confusion on Bud's face, he continued, "Ah—you interpreted that as an indication that I was holding you to it after all."

"Well, yeah," Bud replied. "After all, it was posted as an official schedule."

"Yes, it was, and I understand your interpretation. But think back—can you recall any instance, other than the one we just talked about, where I held you to that initial estimate?"

Bud took some time to ponder Bob's question. "No, no I can't. But I've got to admit that now I'm even more confused than I was before."

Bob smiled. "You see, Bud, it's like this—I've managed a lot of projects in my career. All my experience tells me that, generally speaking, projects just don't finish on time. Oh, I've seen the occasional one that did, but those have been so few and far between that they tend to seem like flukes. The overwhelming majority of projects simply finish late.

"So, knowing what I know, I've done what I could to try to allow for the fact that the estimates people give me aren't worth, excuse me for saying so, a hill of beans. No offense."

"None taken, "Bud responded. "In fact, I agree with you."

"Good. I'm glad. So I've taken to employing a number of different, uh, tactics, in order to make up for this deficiency."

"Like publishing official schedules?"

"Yes, like that," Bob chuckled, "but I prefer to think of them as 'stretch goals.' The idea is to urge people to achieve more than they thought they could.

"That's why I encouraged you to motivate your team to work overtime—to get them to deliver one hundred and ten percent.

"Another thing I regularly do is to pad estimates. For example, when you told me the FutureCash project would take about three months, I automatically multiplied that by a fudge factor. Around here, that factor has traditionally been between 1.5 and 2."

"Are you saying that you actually expected the project to take between four and a half and six months?"

"Yes, that's what I'm saying," Bob replied, "but it seems I may have padded a little enthusiastically in this case."

"I'd say so," Bud confirmed. "At this point, it looks like the software development portion of the project will finish around the sixteen-week mark. Add another week on top of that to account for final testing and documentation, and we should be ready to deploy at seventeen weeks." Bud fiddled with his calculator. "In your terms, that would be a fudge factor of only 1.2."

"Yes, and I'm impressed, as I said before. I think you've got the makings of a fine manager, Bud. It seems that you've been able to motivate people to excel beyond even my expectations, and I congratulate you on that!"

"Well, I appreciate that, Bob, I really do," Bud said. "I'm not sure that's how I would characterize things, though."

"What do you mean?"

"Well, about that overtime, for example—it turned out that, by the time I talked to Ted Russell about the idea of putting in overtime, his people were already doing that. In other words, they motivated themselves."

"Well, even better!" Bob said enthusiastically. "Looks like you've got their loyalty, and that's important, too."

Bob went on before Bud could respond. "I suppose you're wondering why I didn't tell you all this three months ago."

"Well, yes, the thought crossed my mind."

"The thing is," Bob went on, "it's not as easy as you might think to find good managers. One of the ways to discover whether someone has what it takes is to just throw them in and let them sink or swim. Think of it as a test to see if you can deal with adversity and come up with solutions on your own. If I hadn't given you a stretch goal, you might not have been motivated to excel as you have—so I let you believe that the schedule was a bit tighter than it actually was. No hard feelings, I hope."

"No, not at all," Bud replied. "I understand your reasoning. Not sure I agree with it, but I understand what you're saying."

Bud hesitated slightly before deciding to go on. "I was wondering if you've noticed the burndown chart, the one that we've been using to track the progress of the project."

"That big chart down by the developers' space? Yes, I've been monitoring that for a while now. Why do you ask?"

"Well, because I think it's important to emphasize how big a part that chart, and all the data that went into it, played in bringing this project in so close to the deadline."

"I'm glad you mentioned it," Bob said. "It had slipped my mind. Seems to me that the chart is another good example of your ability to motivate the people working under you. It was positively brilliant of you to put that up so that anyone could tell if the project schedule was slipping. After all, as managers we shouldn't be afraid to apply a little pressure from time to time, right?"

Bud forced a smile. He supposed that Bob's perspective on things likely seemed reasonable—to Bob—but couldn't imagine a way to get them both on the same page. Not a simple one, anyway.

Bob continued cheerfully. "Well that's about all I have for you, Bud. I'm glad we had this talk. Just wanted to say thanks, and good work!"

Bud rose and shook the extended hand. "Thanks, Bob."

On the way back to his own office, Bud's thoughts turned to practical matters. Addressing the perspective gap would have to wait—he still had a project to finish.

# 27

The wrap party had long been a tradition at FiscalWare, so it came as no surprise when one was announced to celebrate the completion of the FutureCash project.

The software development team's velocity had held relatively steady, and the project was completed in the middle of the eighteenth week of development. Announcements had been made to the industry press. It was official—FutureCash was a reality.

Bud entered the multi-purpose room, in which these types of events were typically held, to find the party already underway. Most of the people directly involved in the project, plus many others, were in attendance.

Bud stood just inside the doorway for a minute or two, scanning the room, before spotting Ted Russell at the food table.

"Howdy, Ted."

"Oh, hey, Bud!" Ted said, momentarily halting the process of filling his plate with munchables. Seeing Bud eyeing his plate, which was already full to near overflowing with snacks, he added, "What can I say? Free food."

"I was just about to grab a plate myself," Bud said. "Looks good." Bud began heaping it on, although with considerably less ambition than Ted had shown. When he was satisfied, he looked at Ted again and asked, "How about grabbing a table?"

"Suits me."

Winding their way among the celebrants, the two men spotted an empty table in a back corner of the room. Once seated, they talked around bites of finger food.

"I want to thank you again," Bud began, "for all the hard work you and your team did to bring this project in."

"I appreciate that, Bud, I truly do," Ted replied. "It was a good project—probably the best one I've been involved in here, so thank *you*."

Bud smiled and nodded acknowledgement. "I also wanted to ask you about something," he went on.

"Sure—what's that?"

"Do you remember back at the beginning of the project, when we were just starting to talk about the schedule? We had a meeting to talk about my ballpark estimate."

"Yes, I certainly do," Ted replied. "What about it?"

"Well, there's something I wondered about then, and have been meaning to ask you about ever since. Now seemed like a good time."

"OK, I'm intrigued. What is it?"

"Just this. That meeting was about providing an estimate for the project schedule—a pretty mundane task by almost anyone's reckoning—but you seemed positively ecstatic about it. I'd never seen anyone show so much enthusiasm over what most people would consider just so much drudgery. Did I read that wrong?"

Ted paused for quite a while before answering. "No, I think you were right. I suppose you'd like to know why?"

"Yes, I would. That's what I've been wondering about all this time."

"It's pretty simple, really," Ted went on. "You may find it hard to believe this, but it was the first time since I've worked at FiscalWare that anyone asked my opinion about how long the work would take. *My* work."

Bud waited, silently encouraging Ted to elaborate.

"Until then, the standard approach was for someone to come along and inform us—me and the other developers—about how long any given project should take. Then we'd be expected to deliver on time, without having had any say in estimating the work we ourselves were going to do. It was frustrating.

"When you came to me and asked for my help in figuring out a schedule, I was delighted. It was a complete surprise and,

I have to admit, I was practically giddy. So, no you weren't wrong. It was a big deal."

"Wow," Bud said. "I had no idea. Getting your input just seemed like the smart thing to do."

"Seems to have turned out that way, huh? So now that you've brought it up, there's more."

"I've got nothing but time," Bud declared.

"The effect I just described didn't stop with me. All of the other developers on the project let me know, one way and another, that they felt the same way. Remember the second burndown chart they put up? I didn't suggest that—Ursula, Vince and William did that on their own. After that, they couldn't wait to finish tasks and update the chart. I've never seen them happier."

"It seems like a whole lot of enthusiasm over something so simple," Bud remarked. "Got any opinions on what got them so fired up?"

"Isn't it obvious?" Ted asked.

Bud raised his eyebrows and shrugged slightly.

"You're not especially bright for a miracle worker, are you, Bud?" Ted joked. "It's simple—once they made the estimates themselves, they took ownership of the work."

"And we're enthusiastic about work that's truly ours," Bud said, completing the thought.

"Yes, exactly," Ted agreed. "That's how I felt about it anyway, and you can see by their actions that the other developers did too."

"Well, that's what I wanted to ask you about. Thanks for clearing that up."

"My pleasure, chief." Ted's gaze drifted from Bud to just beyond him. "Looks like Bob Harvey's headed this way."

Ted was right. Bud turned in his chair just as Bob arrived and seated himself at their table.

"Gentlemen," Bob said by way of greeting. "Mind if I join you?"

"Have a seat."

"Howdy, Bob. Not at all," Bud replied.

"Good, thanks. Say, Bud, there's something I'd like to ask you about."

"Sure."

"Shall I clear out?" Ted asked.

"No, Ted, please stay. You might as well hear this, too."

Bud and Ted both waited, somewhat anxiously, for Bob to continue.

"Here it is—I just now got the word from sales and marketing—the Phoenix project is a go."

The two men looked at each other, eyebrows raised. The project that Bob had mentioned, code-named Phoenix, had been the subject of many, many conversations around the company for the better part of a year. It was almost stunning to hear that they were actually going to build it.

Bud was the first to break the silence. "Wow, that's a pretty big deal, Bob. Congratulations."

"Congratulations yourself, Bud. The other thing I wanted to tell you is that we'd like for you to manage the project."

Bud was speechless, but eventually managed a nod.

Ted recovered more quickly. "Excellent choice, Bob. If anyone can pull that off, Bud can."

"Yes, I think so, too," Bob concurred. "Now, there's just one thing I want to ask you, Bud, then I'll let you get back to the party."

Bud managed to find his voice. "Sure, Bob. What is it?"

"How long do you think it'll take?"